TYPES OF INTERPRETATION IN THE AESTHETIC DISCIPLINES

Types of Interpretation in the Aesthetic Disciplines

Edited by
Staffan Carlshamre
and Anders Pettersson

McGill-Queen's University Press
Montreal & Kingston · London · Ithaca

ISBN 0-7735-2528-9 (cloth)
ISBN 0-7735-2571-8 (paper)

Legal deposit second quarter 2003
Bibliothèque nationale du Québec

Printed in Canada on acid-free paper.

This book has been published with the help of a grant from the Bank of Sweden Tercentenary Foundation.

McGill-Queen's University Press acknowledges the support of the Canada Council for the Arts for our publishing program. We also acknowledge the financial support of the Government of Canada through the Book Publishing Industry Development Program (BPIDP) for our publishing activities.

National Library of Canada Cataloguing in Publication

Types of interpretation in the aesthetic disciplines / edited by Staffan Carlshamre and Anders Pettersson.

Includes index.
ISBN 0-7735-2528-9 (bound). – ISBN 0-7735-2571-8 (pbk.)

1. Criticism. 2. Interpretation (Philosophy) I. Carlshamre, Staffan II. Pettersson, Anders, 1946-

NX640.T96 2003 700'.1 C2002-905408-7

This book was typeset by Dynagram Inc. in 10/13 Palatino.

Contents

Acknowledgments

The work on this anthology was carried out within the framework of the Stockholm-based interdisciplinary research project "Meaning and Interpretation" ("Mening och tolkning"), led by Professor Dag Prawitz and sponsored by the Bank of Sweden Tercentenary Foundation. This economic backing made it possible for the contributors to meet repeatedly over several years and also to discuss the material, or portions of it, with larger groups of scholars. In addition, the Tercentenary Foundation financed some of our research and supplied us with a publication grant. We are deeply grateful for this generous support.

In April 1999, we discussed a draft of the anthology with two external specialists, Jørgen Dines Johansen and Paisley Livingston, at a two-day seminar in Stockholm. Their detailed comments and criticism influenced the final version of the manuscripts in important respects. We would like to express our gratitude to both of them for their perception and helpfulness.

Sven-Åke Heed, Hans Ruin, Lars-Åke Skalin, and Göran Sonesson took part in the discussions in the anthology group and continuously shared their insights with us. We thank them cordially.

We would also like to say a warm thank you to Pat Shrimpton, who checked our English most expertly.

Penn State University Press has kindly granted permission to reprint three paragraphs from Torsten Pettersson's essay "The Literary Work as a Pliable Entity: Combining Realism and Pluralism," in *Is There a Single Right Interpretation?* ed. Michael Krausz (2002).

Stockholm and Umeå June 2001
Staffan Carlshamre
Anders Pettersson

TYPES OF INTERPRETATION
IN THE AESTHETIC DISCIPLINES

INTRODUCTION

The Multiplicity of Interpretation and the Present Collection of Essays

Anders Pettersson

1. KINDS OF INTERPRETATION

In the course of the twentieth century, interpretation has become of more and more absorbing interest to critics and scholars of literature, art, theatre, and so on. Rightly or not, it has begun to be regarded by many as the centrepiece of the academic study of literature and the arts.

It is only natural, therefore, that the theory of interpretation has come to attract more and more attention both in the aesthetic disciplines themselves and in philosophical aesthetics. With the passage of time, several influential, mutually divergent approaches to the problems of interpretation theory have been worked out and refined – conventionalist, intentionalist, reader-response oriented, deconstructionist, and so on. An extensive literature has accumulated, dealing with problems such as the role of the author's or artist's intentions in interpretation, the determinacy or indeterminacy of meaning, and the possibility of true, or valid, or plausible interpretation.

With relatively few exceptions, the participants in these debates have implicitly understood interpretation to be a definite activity that can be characterized in non-disjunctive terms. It has certainly been evident to all that interpretation is in reality practised in many forms and motivated by varying concerns and convictions. But on the whole, the ambition of theorists of interpretation has nevertheless been to detect and explain *the* logic of interpretation, *the* principles underlying our interpretive practice. The dominant intuition seems to have been that the interpretation of a given artwork constitutes an identifiable, relatively unequivocal task – although a task that is performed in different ways by critics or scholars of diverging persuasions.

However, if one looks carefully at the activities and statements that are normally – i.e., in current everyday and academic usage – referred to as interpretation(s), it should be obvious that they cannot really be understood as attempts to perform the same sort of task, and that their acceptability conditions and so on must therefore vary. This, in turn, is bound to have important consequences for the theory of interpretation. Theorizing that ignores the actual multiplicity of interpretation will lead to unwarranted generalizations. On the other hand, the apparent incompatibility between differing views of interpretation may, in part, be illusory and the effect of merely verbal divergences.

These observations form the starting-point for the present volume. In my introduction, I shall first develop and substantiate the foregoing remarks through a number of more specific observations about modern interpretation theory and the kind of awareness of the multiplicity of interpretation exhibited there. I then conclude with a presentation of the project that has resulted in the writing of the present anthology, and with an introduction to the individual contributions.

The philosophical and critical debate about interpretation of the arts has been particularly lively since the Second World War, and has not least concerned literary interpretation (something which is perhaps natural, considering that literature is the form of art where the existence of a *meaning* to interpret becomes especially obvious). This is particularly true about anglophone criticism and aesthetics – the traditions which form the most important background to our discussions in the anthology.

To recapitulate briefly some key events in a story undoubtedly well known to the reader: The New Criticism of literature was extremely influential in early postwar theorizing about the interpretation of literature, i.e., in the 1940s and 1950s. In opposition to the traditional concentration on author and intended meaning, it made popular the conventionalist idea that the public rules associated with reading have the power to determine the meaning of a work of literature. (The salient texts are a number of contributions by the philosopher Monroe C. Beardsley.)[1] The New Critical standpoint soon provoked a counter-reaction, and the arguments for intentionalism, the view that a work's meaning somehow depends on what its author meant to convey with his or her words, were marshalled by a number of authors, most notably by E.D. Hirsch in his *Validity in Interpretation*

(1967) and later contributions.[2] In the 1960s, however, the belief in the possibility of attaining objectively true interpretations of works of literature and art – a belief held by classical conventionalists and classical intentionalists alike – was already beginning to fade, undermined by theorists insisting on the reader's role in the constitution of literary and artistic meaning. In the course of the 1970s, several influential thinkers with a conventionalist training started to argue that meaning in literature is underdetermined by the linguistic expressions used, which leaves the reader free to fill the vacant semantic space.[3] From the 1970s onwards, then, attention to the reader's role has become ubiquitous in interpretation theory. Many even advocate the radical position that meaning is in fact created by the readers and maintain that all that needs to be said is that readers read in accordance with the expectations instilled into them by the interpretive community to which they belong, or that they use the work, which in itself lacks an essence, in the way they find best.[4] A whole range of intermediate positions can also be found, not least in the current sophisticated debates in anglophone aesthetics.[5]

The analyses just alluded to, while normally both shrewd and imaginative, tend to neglect the circumstance that our interpretive activities are of several basically different kinds. This, I believe, represents a serious limitation in them. The typical theory of interpretation appears to capture the logic of some specific kind of interpretation quite well, but to fail to present a general account of the phenomenon/phenomena, and the participants in the discussion often seem to talk at cross-purposes.

When speaking of different kinds of interpretation of the arts, one should not forget the underlying relationships between the kinds, relationships which motivate the common designation. If one takes a broad view of the creation and enjoyment of art, one could say that the author or artist creates a text or an artwork which the reader or viewer perceives and contemplates. There is a meaning associated with the text or work, and interpretation is the ringing in of that meaning. This manner of speaking is entirely justified as long as one is interested in the very general picture and not really in a detailed comprehension of the phenomena.

The general picture is, however, based on a system of metaphors, and is bound to dissolve on closer inspection.[6] The text or painting does not in reality literally embody a meaning, is not charged with a meaning, or the like. The relationships between physical object and meaning are far more intricate and multifarious than that, and what we call "meaning" in common parlance is not itself a homogeneous entity. Rather, "meaning" is a blanket term covering a multitude of more specific phenomena, and interpretation, the establishment of meaning, must consequently also constitute several enterprises bearing a common name.

In saying this, I am not simply referring to the well-known fact that different critical schools such as Marxism, deconstruction, and new historicism approach literature and art from various starting-points and employ competing theories. I am speaking not of *different ways of performing the same task*, like different ways of painting a door, but of *different tasks*, like the painting of a door and putting a lock on it. Both activities could go by the name of "door modification"; likewise, principally dissimilar activities, answering to palpably different needs and requirements, go by the name of "interpretation."

I shall attempt to substantiate and illustrate these contentions. Let me first, however, emphasize that the heterogeneity of interpretation may be described from many angles and in many fashions. All versions will have drawbacks as well as advantages, and they are bound to rest on suppositions that will seem dubious at least to some. The reader will meet several such descriptions of aspects of the multiplicity of interpretation in the anthology. It is my hope that the existence of genuinely different *kinds* of interpretation, and the importance of taking account of such diversity, will become evident despite the controversial nature of one or the other individual claim.

Just for the sake of this introductory exposition, I should like to introduce a simple tripartite distinction between kinds of interpretation.[7] One common component of what we usually call interpretation is the achievement of a *verbal or visual understanding* of a text or a work of visual art: a basic understanding of the verbal meaning of the words and sentences or of the representational meaning (if any) of the painted surface, the piece of moulded clay, or the like. But interpretation, as we normally comprehend it, undoubtedly comprises other aspects as well. One is the *appreciation* of the work, the global view of the qualities of the work and their import.[8] Thirdly, there are also all sorts of *scholarly or critical investigations* going under the name of interpretation – activities concerned, for example, with the description of the work's structuring or with relating the work to its time, its creator, or its intellectual background. These pursuits are seldom reducible to verbal or visual understanding or to appreciation. The important differences between the three practices or subpractices just mentioned are easily overlooked – not least, perhaps, because scholarly and critical interpretations also build on verbal understanding, and because many critical interpretations suggest appreciations.

2. THE IMPORTANCE OF DISTINGUISHING BETWEEN KINDS OF INTERPRETATION

A theory of interpretation typically fits one type of interpretation to the exclusion of the others. Intentionalism and conventionalism, for example, are perhaps most naturally regarded as competing analyses of the mechanisms responsible for our verbal or visual understanding, i.e., for our establishing a verbal or representational meaning. When we attempt to comprehend such kinds of interpretation as appreciation, where the reader's or viewer's creative imagination must be involved to a high degree, intentionalism and conventionalism are of little help. Conversely, reader-orientated approaches make a great deal of sense where appreciation is concerned but appear unsuitable in accounting for the logic of basic verbal or visual understanding. And if one attempts to take up an intermediate position, one's proposal will typically display not only the strengths but also the weaknesses of the options combined.

To make these observations more concrete, let us take a quick look at a few influential, or once influential, standpoints on meaning and interpretation, beginning with Beardsley. In his *Aesthetics: Problems in the Philosophy of Criticism* (1958), Beardsley emphasizes – with perfect justice, of course – that there is a distinction between what the speaker means by a sentence that he or she utters and what the uttered sentence means in itself: "For what the sentence means depends not on the whim of the individual, and his mental vagaries, but upon public conventions of usage that are tied up with habit patterns in the whole speaking community."[9] Beardsley identifies a critical interpretation with "a statement that purports to declare the 'meaning' of a work of art."[10] He apparently finds it evident that the sentence meaning, not the utterer's meaning, is the "real" meaning, as it were, the only appropriate object of our endeavours to assign meaning. What is more, he obviously thinks that the "public conventions of usage" alluded to are definite enough to settle questions not only about what is commonly called "literal" or "verbal" meaning but also about any question concerning the meaning of a text that is important for literary criticism. It is true that our perceiving of the meaning of the text, as Beardsley understands it, does at some point shade off into something more subjective, into "our complex response to the work."[11] But meaning is a broad notion in Beardsley's analysis – such things as irony, symbolic import, and thematic content all fall within its scope[12] – and Beardsley certainly implies that interpretation is, in principle, a true or false "declaration" of that meaning.[13]

Beardsley's approach leaves many things ordinarily seen as interpretations unaccounted for. It appears difficult to deny, for example, that some interpretations are best understood as attempts to highlight certain features of a work, or to indicate or recommend a certain way of apprehending the work. (Otto Pächt's van Eyck criticism in his 1989 monograph – described in Margaretha Rossholm Lagerlöf's article below – appears to fall into that category.) Interpretations of this kind are no doubt normally *restricted* by public conventions of usage, but cannot reasonably be thought of as being *wholly determined* by them. Or, to consider an example of another type: some interpretations are naturally understood as attempted reconstructions of how the author or artist saw his or her work. (For example, in an essay by Hartmut Binder about the background of Kafka's "The Judgement," Binder's identification of the theme of the story may be such a reconstruction. See my suggestion in my own essay in this volume.) Attempts to define how an author or artist intended a text or a painting to be understood are certainly empirical statements, true or false in principle. Public conventions of usage furnish important evidence about such intentions, but they cannot possibly *wholly determine* their correct description. Thus Beardsley's analysis appears relevant only for a portion of what is in fact normally seen as interpretation, and this is the simple point to which I want to draw attention. (It is another question, which I leave aside here, whether or not conventionalism of Beardsley's brand offers an adequate analysis of the kind or kinds of interpretation where it constitutes a serious possibility.)

A person sympathetic to Beardsley's analysis might wish to counter these objections by declaring that it is improper to talk about interpretation in the kinds of cases used as counter-examples against Beardsley. But taking that position would, in my view, be to arbitrarily exclude important parts of the actual polysemy of the concept of interpretation.[14] And moreover, whether defensible or not in itself, such a stipulation would not remove the real problem with Beardsley's account. For by presenting it as an analysis of interpretation *tout court,* Beardsley gives an exaggerated and consequently misleading idea of its possible scope. He aspires to explain the logic of interpretation in general, but if we believe in his analysis we will misconstrue many of the things normally called interpretation.

The criticism just levelled at Beardsley's analysis could be directed – with minor modifications, but with equal justice – at practically every significant analysis of interpretation. Take for example E.D. Hirsch, Beardsley's most important adversary during the late 1960s and early 1970s, and his well-known distinction between meaning and significance:

> *Meaning* is that which is represented by a text; it is what the author meant with his use of a particular sign sequence; it is what the signs represent. *Significance,* on the other hand, names a relationship between that meaning and a person, or a conception, or a situation, or indeed anything imaginable.[15]

According to Hirsch, meaning in this sense, what he calls "verbal meaning,"[16] is the "exclusive object" of interpretation.[17] The analysis makes it easy for him to account for part of what is normally called "interpretation" – at least for reconstructions of the author's meaning. On the other hand, the definition excludes many other activities normally designated by that name, redescribing them as "criticism," the pursuit of significance.[18]

It is no doubt often relevant, in a literary or artistic context, to consider the factor that Hirsch calls "meaning" or "verbal meaning." Recovering its content in connection with a given work may, not least, be important from a critical or scholarly point of view. By tying the prestigious concepts "meaning" and "interpretation" to just these two denotata, however, Hirsch relegates all other kinds of (what is usually called) meaning and interpretation to another plane and implies that they are of secondary importance only. If one is aware of the multitude of ordinary uses of "meaning," one can perceive clearly that Hirsch's analysis builds on a partisan, persuasive definition of "interpretation" (and of "meaning").

Richard Rorty's outline analysis of interpretation in "The Pragmatist's Progress" (1992), very different in content, supplies a more modern example of an analysis which elevates a special variety of meaning and interpretation to an unduly privileged position. In Rorty's view, a text can be understood in different ways, and it does not have an essence that is separable from the way in which the text appears to different readers. There is consequently nothing to appeal to over and above the reactions of the text's readers, who encounter the text as it emerges in their respective individual perspectives.

It is only natural, then, for Rorty to criticize Umberto Eco's distinction between *interpreting* and *using* a text – a distinction reminiscent of Hirsch's dichotomy between interpretation (the establishing of meaning) and criticism (the pursuit of significance). "This, of course, is a distinction we pragmatists do not wish to make," says Rorty. "On our view, all anybody ever does with anything is use it. Interpreting something, knowing it, penetrating to its essence, and so on are all just various ways of describing some process of putting it to work."[19] Rorty also seems to wish to deny that there are privileged ways of using a text. He urges us to "just distinguish between uses by different people for different purposes."[20]

I do not wish to take Rorty's more philosophical observations up for discussion here. I would simply like to point out that when Rorty describes interpretation ("reading"), he is in reality characterizing a specific variety, namely, appreciation – the personal, more or less creative and subjective, overall understanding of a text: "Reading texts is a matter of reading them in the light of other texts, people, obsessions, bits of information, or what have you, and then seeing what happens."[21] Interpretation focused on the author's or artist's intentions, or on the verbal meaning of a poem or the representational content of a painting, cannot, however, be construed so liberally: some kinds of bits of information will inevitably be relevant to the project, others not. As I see it, Rorty's analysis gives a one-sided and hence misleading picture of reading and interpretation. (Incidentally, this strikes me as surprising and unnecessary, since attention to interpretation's multifariousness in no way undermines, but rather lends support to, Rorty's main idea that all that exists in connection with texts is "uses by different people for different purposes.")

There is, certainly, more awareness of the multiplicity of interpretation in current interpretation theory than the Beardsley, Hirsch, and Rorty examples would lead one to believe. Several contemporary theorists stress that interpretation of the arts may be of many different kinds; I shall come to this soon. Nevertheless, the multiplicity of interpretation goes almost unnoticed even in much advanced contemporary theory, and its consequences are mostly neglected.

In the intentionalist camp the most sophisticated debates about literary interpretation in recent years have been carried out between so-called "actual" and "hypothetical" intentionalists. Roughly speaking, actual intentionalists hold that our attempts to identify the meaning of a literary text do in reality constitute an attempt to identify the communicative intentions of its author. The hypothetical intentionalist maintains that they constitute, instead, an attempt to arrive at the best possible hypothesis about those intentions that is available to a suitably equipped reader. Meaning, the object of interpretation, becomes either what the author meant, or what the competent reader must reasonably take him or her to mean.

As before, I do not wish to enter into the real matter of contention, just point to the fact that awareness of the multiplicity of interpretation is virtually absent from this highly contemporary and professional debate. Jerrold Levinson, for example, who coined the term "hypothetical intentionalism" and is the foremost current champion of the stance,[22] writes in a recent contribution:

> The issues surrounding the interpretation of literary texts and the relation of that activity to authors' intentions in writing such texts are of long standing and show little sign of being settled anytime soon. ... The view I defend concerning the interpretation and meaning of literary works is strictly neither intentionalism nor anti-intentionalism, as those are usually delineated, but what might be called *hypothetical* (or constructive) *intentionalism*.[23]

Here, hypothetical intentionalism is clearly presented as a theory about *the* interpretation of literary works understood as a single, in a sense homogeneous, activity. *Prima facie*, however, it seems clear that an analysis of the Levinsonian kind must leave much of what is commonly called interpretation uncovered. It cannot, for example, reasonably account for interpretation of the kinds illustrated by the Pächt and Binder examples alluded to above. For constructing and advocating a certain favoured way of apprehending the work (as in the Pächt case) cannot be identical with forming as good a hypothesis as possible about the author's communicative intentions. And as regards the attempted reconstruction of how the author or artist saw his or her work (the Binder case), it must obviously be actual intentionalism, not Levinson's hypothetical intentionalism, that supplies us with the correct description of its logic. What Levinson's analysis addresses is, in reality, the understanding of the verbal meaning of a text. Such verbal understanding is certainly a key issue where the theory of interpretation is concerned, but verbal understanding does not constitute interpretation *simpliciter,* or even interpretation in the most paradigmatic sense of the word.

Let me amplify. In the essay just quoted, Levinson implicitly understands (interpretation as the recovery of meaning, and) meaning as verbal meaning. Meaning of all other kinds – meaning in all other senses of the word – is regarded as secondary and of less importance. For that reason, the important variety of interpretation that I call here "appreciation" (the personal, somewhat creative and subjective, overall understanding of a text) more or less disappears from view. True, at a certain point Levinson observes that one way of construing the meaning of a literary text is to see it as what he calls "ludic meaning," a category comprising "any meanings that can be attributed to either a brute text (a word-sequence-in-a-language) or a text-as-utterance, by virtue of interpretive play constrained by only the loosest requirements of plausibility, intelligibility, or interest."[24] This no doubt refers to meaning produced by personal, creative understanding, though Levinson (probably thinking mainly of poststructuralist or deconstructionist extravagancies) caricatures that kind of meaning ascription. He also remarks – and I fully agree – that ludic meaning cannot be "the fundamental meaning of literary texts, if only because it presupposes such in order to get off the ground."[25] Nevertheless, what Levinson somewhat tendentiously describes as ludic meaning is indubitably a crucial factor in some quite central variants of the activities that are normally called interpretation. The ordinary concept of interpretation, simply cannot be tied to the recovery of verbal meaning in the rather direct and unequivocal way that Levinson seems to envisage.

The result of the Levinsonian moves just described is an analysis which comes close to Hirsch's in its handling of the multiplicity of meaning and interpretation. Levinson's analysis is obviously perfectly relevant (again, I will not raise the question of the proposal's adequacy) for the central case of verbal meaning. Nevertheless, I would say that it gives a misleading idea of interpretation, since it portrays interpretation as, centrally, the attempted recovery of authorial meaning and describes other varieties as more or less secondary and irresponsible.

This does not mean that awareness of the multiplicity of interpretation is entirely absent from the discussions between actual and hypothetical intentionalists. It surfaced in Levinson's references to ludic meaning, and multiplicity is also sometimes alluded to in the contributions of Gary Iseminger, an important advocate of actual intentionalism and thus one of Levinson's main opponents. Iseminger sometimes implies that there are several "kinds of interpretive statements"[26] or emphasizes that his analysis is only meant to hold for "at least some kinds of interpretive statements."[27] But Iseminger makes no real use of the insight either; the quoted phrases practically sum up what he has to say about that side of the matter in the contributions in question.

I believe that part of the dissension between actual and hypothetical intentionalism may in fact be verbal. It is actually, up to a point at least, possible to construe actual and hypothetical intentionalism as true for different kinds of interpretation. In that connection, it is important to understand that sameness of interpretive object does not necessarily imply sameness of interpretive task. Interpretation directed to the author's or artist's intentions may be undertaken for quite different reasons. Thus, as we have seen, according to some literary theorists verbal understanding is geared to the establishment of the author's intention. At the same time, however, historical understanding of an artwork (the motives behind it, and so on) clearly presupposes an understanding of the intentions of an author or artist (think, once again, of Binder's discussion of the theme of "The Judgement"). Hence we may, especially in a scholarly context, wish to recover an author's or artist's communicative intentions whether or not we believe that such intentions are constitutive of verbal or representational meaning. *Verbal or visual understanding* and *scholarly recovery of the originator's communicative intentions* are simply two partly different tasks.

To the best of my knowledge, this fact has never been thematized in the current discussions between hypothetical intentionalists (like Levinson) and those who stress, in different ways, the importance of the author's or artist's actual intentions (like Iseminger). I do not believe that the controversy between actual and hypothetical intentionalists would evaporate if the distinction between verbal understanding and scholarly recovery of intention were given due consideration. Presumably, divergences in the analysis of verbal understanding are also at issue. But possibly the dissension between the two camps is *to some extent* illusory. It is conceivable that Levinson would be able to accept the interpretive relevance of actual authorial intentions in specific contexts (while still arguing for their irrelevance in others), since that would hardly force him to modify his standpoint more than marginally.

3. KINDS OF INTERPRETATION: SOME EARLIER ANALYSES

We have already encountered critics or philosophers who point to the multiplicity of meaning or import assignment. Hirsch's distinction between interpretation and criticism is a case in point, and the more incidental remarks just quoted from Levinson and Iseminger provide another example. More importantly, the fundamental heterogeneity of interpretive activities has been emphatically thematized by some theorists. Some have drawn an analogy between different interpretations and descriptions of the same object seen from different perspectives.[28] Others have stressed that interpretations may be governed by widely differing interests, and that the object which they ostensively seek to unveil, "the meaning" of the work of art, is not in fact a definite, objectively recoverable entity.[29] The idea that there are fundamentally different *types* of interpretations that may differ both in the kind of object they are directed at and in the kind of purpose motivating the activity is, however, relatively recent. The earliest contribution in this spirit that I know of is a perceptive article from 1984 by Göran Hermerén, "Interpretation: Types and Criteria." Hermerén observes that theorists of interpretation are prone to talk of interpretation in general terms and to claim, for example, "that interpretations always (or never) can be 'true' or 'correct,' that they always (or never) contain or imply important truths about human life, that they always (or never) result in explications of a certain kind of 'meaning,' that they are always (or never) concerned with the intentions of the person whose text or action is interpreted, or that the interpreted text in the interpretation is always (or never) applied to the interpreter's own situation."[30] He then goes on to argue that there are a large number of methodologically different types of interpretations. Even where something as relatively circumscribed as the interpretation of texts is concerned, Hermerén discerns at least eleven significantly different types: emendation, linguistic (semantic) interpretation, interpretation of the author's meaning, interpretation of intentions, psychological extrapolation, application (demonstration of relevance), theoretical (or allegorical) reinterpretation, interpretation of symptoms, historic reconstruction, augmentation of value (aesthetic interpretation), and performance.[31] He concludes, reasonably enough, that "interpretation is used about many different kinds of statements and activities. Thus there are important differences between what is referred to as 'interpretations.' The common, cavalier assumption that the same sort of predicate – be it 'true,' 'correct,' or 'plausible' – can be used about *all* sorts of interpretations then becomes doubtful, to say the least."[32]

Hermerén's aim is to demonstrate the multiplicity of interpretation and the necessity of taking it into account when constructing an interpretation theory. It is therefore understandable that Hermerén wishes to stress how many different types of interpretation we may in fact distinguish (and that he considers the interpretation not only of texts but also of dreams, events, actions, etc.).[33] His description of eleven separate types of textual interpretation is altogether functional when seen in that perspective. On the other hand, if one is looking for an overall understanding of interpretation one is bound to find it unenlightening, and consequently unconvincing, to see interpretation broken down into eleven separate activities whose mutual relations are left unclear. It is easy to feel that something has been missed: the inner relationships motivating the common designation.[34]

Richard Shusterman's *The Object of Literary Criticism*, which contains an interesting chapter on the logic of interpretation, appeared in the same year as Hermerén's article. In the chapter in question Shusterman, too, is specifically concerned with emphasizing the heterogeneity of interpretive approaches and the impossibility of subsuming them all under one unitary interpretative logic.

Shusterman's focus is not really on interpretive statements but on interpretive activities or practices ("games"). However, in much the same vein as Hermerén, he insists that there is "no one logic of interpretation, but rather many logics of interpretation. Different critics play different interpretative 'games' with different sets of rules or 'logics' implicit in the games they practice."[35]

A special feature of Shusterman's analysis is his description of the conflict between various interpretive approaches as a struggle for life:

> Interpretation is not *one* game but a *family* of games; and as in other families, there are sibling rivalries where the value and even legitimacy of certain members of the family are bitterly contested. It is not the job of the philosopher of criticism, as analyst, to award the birthright. Having identified and analyzed the various interpretative games, he must let them justify themselves, as they have justified and must justify themselves, in actual

critical practice. Having distinguished between the different species, he must rely on the survival of the fittest.[36]

Though Shusterman does not explicitly say any such thing, the biological imagery makes it sound as if rationality does not enter into the picture when it comes to choosing among different interpretive schemes. Such a view would seem difficult to uphold. It is also important to point out that, though indeed there are many different "games" that we can and do play as readers/viewers, critics, and scholars, the interpretations proffered within their respective frames often do not contradict each other, and so the games often are not really competitors. Nothing prevents us from viewing Manet's *A Bar at the Folies-Bergère* for enjoyment without applying any specific analytical tools, and then also to study it professionally (its causal background, its structure, its themes) or to suggest a strong, innovative reading of the painting (see the examples discussed in the last section of my "Five Kinds of Literary and Artistic Interpretation," below).

Another publication from the 1980s which explicitly points to the multiplicity of interpretation is Annette Barnes's *On Interpretation: A Critical Analysis* (1988). Barnes's brief last chapter, "Interpreting and Diverse Critical Activities," is in fact largely devoted to emphasizing that "interpreting is irreducibly pluralistic: fundamentally diverse critical activities count as interpreting."[37] The critical activities that Barnes has in mind are, first and foremost, those of assessing what artworks "represent, describe, exemplify, or express."[38] Barnes's account is somewhat abstract, which makes it difficult to compare it in any detail with the view of the multiplicity of interpretation which I presented earlier. Personally, I find Barnes's descriptions of critical activities rather narrow, and I doubt her claim that "while not all interpretations need be statements, nor all interpreting involve stating, a substantial amount of critical interpreting in the arts does involve this"[39] – as I see it, few varieties of interpretation result in true-or-false statements.[40] Nevertheless, I regard Barnes's careful formulations about the multiplicity of interpretation as being basically correct as far as they go and as an important expression of the stance.

Three books from recent years where the multiplicity of interpretation is emphatically foregrounded are Patrick Colm Hogan's *On Interpretation: Meaning and Inference in Law, Psychoanalysis, and Literature* (1996), Robert Stecker's *Artworks: Definition Meaning Value* (1997), and Paul Thom's *Making Sense: A Theory of Interpretation* (2000).[41]

Hogan's work is based on the conviction (which I share) that many quite different things are called "meaning" in connection with texts and other artworks, and that "interpretation," standing for the recovery of meaning, is thus a blanket term covering a multitude of profoundly different, but often perfectly legitimate, pursuits.

Therefore, according to Hogan,

> … it is important to say whether one is going to examine individual readers' affective responses, the personal/biographical associations of the author, the changing views of critics as historically and socially "situated," self-conscious authorial descriptive intent (as given in, say, truth-conditions), and so forth. It is important to stipulate this. But it is senseless to debate which activity is "really" interpretation, which object is "really" meaning.[42]

Hogan argues that all existing meanings are "intents" (a term by which he seems to refer to, approximately, mental states or mental contents),[43] and he sees interpretation as being "inference to intent"[44] guided by normal rational principles. Hogan also conceives of interpretation in the arts as being heterogeneous: according to him, it may be aimed at various kinds of meaning, none of which are really privileged.[45] Hogan finds, however, that one kind of intent plays an especially distinctive role in literature: "authorial aesthetical intent."[46] Using a terminology borrowed from classical Indian aesthetics, Hogan describes aesthetical intent as "the complex of rasadhvani that an author experiences in deciding his/her work to be aesthetically 'right', to be finished (or, at least, to be 'finished enough')."[47]

I would like here to pass over the issue of the ontology of meaning. As regards the nature of interpretation, however, I find it obvious that much interpretation of the arts (in the normal sense of the word "interpretation") is in fact not a *reconstruction of mental facts* but a *forging of experience*, a constructive and to some extent subjective activity. This applies, above all, to what is here called "appreciation": it must be characterized as creative rather than explicative or descriptive. That aspect appears to be absent from Hogan's system, which is built wholly around the reconstruction of intents.

The multiplicity of interpretation also plays an important role in Robert Stecker's *Artworks*. Stecker writes:

> Because we value art, we typically approach artworks in order to appreciate them, but this can be done in more than one way. Thus we may seek to

> appreciate a work as would a contemporary of its author, or we may seek to appreciate it in a way that makes it relevant to concerns or ways of thinking of our own time. Also, our appreciation may focus on different properties or functions of a work. ... Because we appreciate and understand works in different ways, we interpret with different *aims*. Typically the aim with which we interpret is determined by the way in which we hope to appreciate a work, but there is one exception, and that is when we seek to understand some aspect of [a] work for the sake of understanding alone.
>
> The standard of acceptability for interpretations is relative to aim. An interpretation that would be unacceptable if it were an attempt to understand the artist's intentions may be a perfectly acceptable attempt to make a work relevant to contemporary concerns. The recognition of this, along with the fact that people interpret with different aims, allows for the resolution of many traditional problems about interpretation.[48]

The view of the multiplicity of interpretation put forward in Stecker's penetrating and impressive book has several important points in common with the one advocated here. As the quotation demonstrates, however, Stecker's view of interpretation is almost exclusively focused on appreciation, the reading/viewing of literature/art for aesthetic or artistic satisfaction. Certainly, the enhancement of our appreciation is sometimes seen as the genuine *raison d'être* of criticism of literature and art, but that idea in itself might be disputed. And, more importantly, an interpretation by a critic cannot normally be understood as having as its aim the reporting of his or her own appreciation of the work. A publicly presented interpretation is possibly sometimes merely a recommendation of a particular way of viewing the work,[49] with an attendant presumption of some sort of wider significance, but hardly ever just an autobiographical statement. For these reasons, I believe that it is important to avoid the identification, or near-identification, of interpretation with appreciation.

At one point Stecker seems to allow us to glimpse the existence of academic interpretation that is not focused on the suggestion of appreciative readings. I am thinking of his observation that we sometimes "seek to understand some aspect of [a] work for the sake of understanding alone."[50] But even if one takes this as an allusion to scholarly interpretation – which may be an over-interpretation – Stecker must be said to have downplayed the importance of interpretation that is not primarily aesthetically orientated: such interpretation has in fact an overwhelmingly massive presence in scholarship and criticism. What I miss when I look at Stecker's picture of interpretation from the perspective of the more empirical aesthetic disciplines (literary studies, art history, and so on), is first and foremost an awareness of the widely varied methodological contexts within which interpretation functions in these disciplines.

If understood as referring to scholarly interpretation, the remark also fails to capture the aims of most such interpretation. The recovery of the originator's intentions, or the analysis of the work's inner structuring, for example, are not normally undertaken just for the sake of arriving at a good idea of the intention or structure. Typically, they form part of critical or scholarly attempts to solve historical or theoretical problems whose importance is only distantly related to appreciation proper, and the character of the interpretations will to a large extent be determined by that role. (Consider the examples of van Eyck criticism in Margaretha Rossholm Lagerlöf's essay below.)

In the theory of interpretation presented in *Making Sense*, Thom's insistence on the possibility of providing a unified analysis of interpretation is perhaps more likely to attract attention than his description of the multiplicity of interpretation, but the latter element is also quite conspicuous. Thom's most general definition of "interpretation" says that an interpretation "is a view of an object that purports to make sense of it by representing it in a particular way."[51] The talk of objects, representations, and ways of sense-making then also opens the way for the distinguishing of different types of interpretation: "The differences between these types arise from differences in the object (nature or art), the medium of representation (discourse or action), the point of representation (understanding or imaginative development), and the kind of governing concept (explanation, representation, expression, etc.)."[52]

Many of the kinds of interpretation that fall under Thom's broad general definition are of little interest in my context: the interpretation of dreams, for example, or the performing of a play, or parodies.[53] I am dealing with what Thom calls "critical interpretation" and tends to see as a kind of its own: "Some kinds of interpretation have a characteristic sort of object and a characteristic sort of governing concept. Let's focus on one such kind – critical interpretation, with its characteristic objects (artworks) and its characteristic array of governing concepts drawn from various critical discourses."[54] Thom mentions, as if it were noteworthy, Barnes's idea that not "even critical interpretations all belong to a single kind," without either endorsing it or objecting to it.[55] But in fact he himself seems, at one stage, to classify literary and artistic interpretation as different kinds, for he says: "We distinguish different kinds of interpretation according to whether they have ... different types of objects; for example, we are accustomed to distinguishing textual interpretation from the interpretation of art or nature, and so on."[56]

One cannot really say that Thom distinguishes between types of interpretation of literature or art. But he clearly differentiates between kinds of interpretation, and it would have been easy for him, using the conceptual apparatus that he has already introduced, to break up critical interpretation into a number of sub-kinds. For interpretation of literature and art can have different objects – e.g., texts or paintings. It can use representations of various types – thought representations as in silent reading, verbal representations as in a book of art history, and so on.[57] The governing concepts, and thus the point of interpreting, may also vary – as they no doubt do in what I called verbal or visual understanding as compared with appreciation or with diverse sorts of scholarly or critical investigations.

Judging from the above, the multiplicity of interpretation, even the diversity of the interpretation of literature and art, may appear to be a well-established fact. Yet I believe that such an impression is incorrect. While interpretation's multifariousness has been pointed to in several well-known contributions to interpretation theory, it has normally figured there as a side-issue, and actual theorizing about interpretation has all too often proceeded without taking any account of the complications that it represents.

It is instructive, in this connection, to peruse a recent anthology edited by Joseph Margolis and Tom Rockmore, *The Philosophy of Interpretation* (1999). I would say that only one of the twelve contributors, Jorge J.E. Gracia, makes extensive use of distinctions between types of interpretation in his analysis.[58] David Novitz and Paul Thom both refer to such distinctions in passing, which is what their respective contexts require.[59] Peter Lamarque notes that interpretation takes many forms but regards literary interpretation as if it were in fact unitary, which seems less than adequate given the problem discussed, namely, the object-groundedness or imputedness of interpretive properties.[60] Noël Carroll,[61] Tom Rockmore,[62] and Joseph Margolis[63] all speak of the interpretation of texts as if it were all of one kind, unjustifiably as I see it, though the point is perhaps not so important in

Rockmore's case. In Margolis and Rockmore's introduction, and in the remaining four contributions (by Stein Haugom Olsen, Michael Krausz, F.R. Ankersmit, and Cecilia Tohaneanu), the multiplicity problem is not really relevant. All in all, this important anthology does not seem to me to indicate that the diversity of the interpretation of literature and art is a well-known and clearly appreciated fact.

4. THE PRESENT COLLECTION OF ESSAYS

The idea of making a collective effort to point out and analyse the multiplicity of types of interpretation was launched within the framework of the Swedish interdisciplinary research program "Meaning and Interpretation" ("Mening och tolkning") in 1995, and eventually a group of people interested in the theme came together and started planning an anthology on the subject. The group convened at irregular intervals, mostly four or five times a year, from 1995 to 1999, to discuss questions concerning interpretation and its typology and, later, the first and second drafts of the individual contributions to the anthology.

Apart from this introduction and Staffan Carlshamre's closing remarks, the anthology comprises five essays. Despite the underlying focus on interpretation of the arts, more general questions surrounding interpretation are broached in several of the contributions.

Torsten Pettersson's "What Is an Interpretation?" is devoted to answering two of the most general questions in the area: "What is considered to be an interpretation in Western culture in our time?" and "What types of interpretation can be usefully distinguished and what are their characteristics?" In the essay, Pettersson strives to capture the content normally associated with the concept of interpretation, but on some points he also suggests stipulations that he finds reasonable. Pettersson distinguishes between the *interpretation of human activities or products*, the *interpretation of the physical world*, and *interpretation in the sense of the performance of an artwork or the like*. He describes interpretation in the first, aesthetically most important sense as "a wittingly produced coherent conceptual representation of the activities or products of sentient beings" which "focuses on elements which the interpreter takes to be poorly understood by the addressee and attempts to clarify their meaning or function." Throughout the essay, he consistently motivates the details of his formulations and differentiates interpretation from different but related cultural practices.

The main object of my own contribution, "Five Kinds of Literary and Artistic Interpretation," is to make more concrete how the legitimate intellectual demands on interpretations may vary according to the interests and aims behind the interpretation, the "type" to which it belongs. Using scholarly or critical writings about Kafka's "The Judgement" and Manet's *A Bar at the Folies-Bergère* as material, I characterize and exemplify a number of significantly different varieties of interpretation. My "typology" – whose ambitions are pedagogical rather than strictly taxonomical – takes the general purposes behind the interpretation as its point of departure. In the essay, I stress the difference between ordinary reading or viewing on the one hand, aimed at enjoyment of the work, and scholarly or critical explication – typically concentrated on clarifying the work's structure, background, or effects – on the other. This forms the basis for reasoned distinctions between *reconstruction* and *assimilation* (where ordinary reading or viewing is concerned), and between such scholarly or critical interpretive practices as *retrieval of intention, structural analysis,* and *explication of focal aspects* (interpretation in the most paradigmatic sense).

Göran Rossholm starts from a broad concept of interpretation safely entrenched in common usage. He then describes what he considers to be "the major ramifications" of the concept. The ramification metaphor – on which Rossholm also plays in the title of his essay, "The Tree of Interpretation" – is amply justified by two extensive tree diagrams summarizing Rossholm's chief distinctions. For Rossholm introduces and explains a number of partly original divisions of interpretations or features of such – for example, into factual, counterfactual, and afactual interpretations, or into referential and substantial incombinability among interpretations. Moreover, he underlines that "nuclear" interpretations may be incorporated into larger justificatory complexes, and also pays heed to this circumstance in his system of distinctions. Rossholm's interest is focused on what he calls "qualified" interpretations – interpretations which go beyond indisputable fact and may conflict with other equally well motivated interpretations – especially on *qualified aesthetic interpretation,* which he finally characterizes as *afactual interpretations of artworks, without truth value but with referential rivals.*

While Torsten Pettersson, Göran Rossholm, and I present more or less elaborated typological sketches, Staffan Carlshamre's "Types of Types of Interpretation" begins with the observation that such typologies may be built up along very different lines. One may offer a classification registering distinctions that are somehow already present in *linguistic usage* (Carlshamre points to Torsten Pettersson's contribution as an example), or one that is "based on an *empirical classification*," i.e., discriminates between actual interpretations with the help of certain preferred criteria (like my own). A third possibility is to concentrate on *mapping the logical space* occupied by interpretations – which can be said to be the aim of Göran Rossholm's article and of Carlshamre's own essay. Carlshamre observes that an interpretation always departs from something manifest and goes to something hidden, and he constructs and reflects upon a clustered list of kinds of entities that may play these respective roles. Carlshamre then proceeds to supplement his outline of a classificatory framework with a discussion of the multiplicity and the distinctiveness of aesthetic interpretation. In that context, he proposes a distinction between *readings* (and the elaboration of readings) and *claims* (and the justification of claims). He also offers an extended discussion of the role (or lack of it) of authorial intention in aesthetic interpretation and of the motivation for that role.

In her essay, "Interpreting Visual Art: Performance and Articulation," Margaretha Rossholm Lagerlöf emphasizes the centrality of aesthetic experience also in connection with the scholarly interpretation of art while she argues, objecting to some of the other essays in the volume, that statements about aesthetic meaning – what I have here called appreciations – carry with them both claims of validity and risks of failure. What she criticizes is, not least, the impulse to separate the rational framework of scholarly interpretation sharply and definitely from involvement and feeling. In her analysis, the various components of an elaborate scholarly interpretation are intimately interrelated, not just complementary, and they comprise both truth-claims and subjectivity.

In the course of her essay, Rossholm Lagerlöf introduces and discusses a series of contributions to the criticism of two van Eyck paintings, the *Van der Paele Madonna* and the *Arnolfini Portrait*. She demonstrates the role played by the scholar's subjectivity in his or her analyses of the paintings, tracing it back to the immediate visual response which already inevitably underlies our responses to a work of visual art.

The contributors were, by and large, given the liberty to decide how they would treat the theme of types of interpretation. Despite this, and despite the different agendas of the individual essays, this overview of the contents should have clearly shown that the anthology has a palpable thematic unity. In his concluding remarks, "Some Metareflections," to which I refer the reader without summarizing them here, Staffan Carlshamre elaborates this further and also endeavours to place the questions we discuss in a wider philosophical perspective.

Insistence on the multiplicity of interpretation should not be understood as a sceptical or relativistic stance. It is true that relativistic conclusions *can* be drawn from it – like the argument by Shusterman cited earlier – but as the works by Hermerén, Barnes, Hogan, Stecker, and Thom illustrate, that is not necessary. Nor is it, perhaps, natural. Indeed, if the label "interpretation" does in fact cover a multitude of intellectual tasks, and if quite different logical or empirical demands are warranted in the different cases, *only consideration of this multiplicity can make successful rational discussion of interpretations possible.* For if the situation is as described, attempts to introduce all-embracing rules for assessing interpretations must fail, and through their failure they are likely to strengthen current scepticism about the role of reason in interpretation.

At the same time, it is important to emphasize that attention to the multiplicity of interpretation can only be one element in a theory of interpretation. It does not, in itself, provide us with any comprehensive view of meaning assignment. Nor does it have a necessary association with any specific perspective on art, value, mind, and so on, since it is compatible with practically each and every philosophical position. Thus the multiplicity claim does not in itself represent a *substantive* aesthetic, interpretive, or philosophical insight. Consideration of the multiplicity of interpretation should be understood as being merely a necessary prerequisite for, or part of, such insight.

Writings on interpretation abound. This contribution to the discussion is first and foremost intended to demonstrate the diversity of interpretations in the arts and the complexity consequently required of an adequate theory of interpretation. We hope that the concerted effort to highlight this diversity and its implications will heighten the awareness of the problem and its significance. Perhaps the anthology, with its interdisciplinary character, may also help to bridge the deplorable gap between discussions of interpretation in philosophical aesthetics and in the individual aesthetic disciplines.

NOTES

1 I am thinking especially of Beardsley's and William Wimsatt's "The Intentional Fallacy " (1946), in Wimsatt, *The Verbal Icon* (Lexington: University of Kentucky Press, 1954), but also of Beardsley's reasoning about meaning and interpretation in *Aesthetics: Problems in the Philosophy of Criticism* (New York: Harcourt, Brace and World, 1958) and in his later book, *The Possibility of Criticism* (Detroit: Wayne State University Press, 1970).

2 E.D. Hirsch, Jr, *Validity in Interpretation* (New Haven: Yale University Press, 1967).

3 As, e.g., Wolfgang Iser in *Der implizite Leser: Kommunikationsformen des Romans von Bunyan bis Beckett* (München: Wilhelm Fink, 1972) – published in an English translation in 1974 as *The Implied Reader: Patterns of Communication in Prose Fiction from Bunyan to Beckett* (Baltimore and London: Johns Hopkins University Press) – and Jonathan Culler in *Structuralist Poetics: Linguistics and the Study of Literature* (London: Routledge and Kegan Paul, 1975).

4 See, e.g., Stanley Fish, *Is There a Text in This Class? The Authority of Interpretive Communities* (Cambridge, Mass. and London: Harvard University Press, 1980) and Richard Rorty, "The Pragmatist's Progress," in Umberto Eco et al., *Interpretation and Overinterpretation*, ed. Stefan Collini (Cambridge: Cambridge University Press, 1992).

5 Varieties of intentionalism and conventionalism still play an important part in these discussions. The contributions by Levinson and Iseminger mentioned in the next section are two examples of contemporary, refined intentionalism. Thinkers of a basically conventionalist persuasion have, for their part, confronted the intentionalist backlash and/or developed more complex conventionalist positions. See, e.g., George Dickie and W. Kent Wilson's "The Intentional Fallacy: Defending Beardsley," *Journal of Aesthetics and Art Criticism* 53 (1995) and Stephen Davies,"Relativism in Interpretation," *Journal of Aesthetics and Art Criticism* 53 (1995), esp. 9–10.

6 I am thinking of the so-called "conduit metaphor," first described by Michael Reddy. See his article "The Conduit Metaphor – A Case of Frame Conflict in Our Language about Language," in Andrew Ortony, ed., *Metaphor and Thought* (Cambridge: Cambridge University Press, 1986).

7 In my own contribution to this anthology, the essay "Five Kinds of Literary and Artistic Interpretation," I suggest a slightly more elaborated system of distinctions.

8 The concept of appreciation has an evaluative aspect, and it is natural to wish to uphold a distinction between interpretation and evaluation. I

have nevertheless decided to use "appreciation" here, since I can find no natural alternative to the word. However, it should be remembered throughout that in using "appreciation" I am not referring to the forming of explicit value-judgments.

9 Beardsley is quoted from Monroe C. Beardsley, *Aesthetics: Problems in the Philosophy of Criticism*, 2nd ed. (Indianapolis and Cambridge: Hackett Publishing Company, 1981), here 25.

10 Ibid., 9.

11 Ibid., 419.

12 Cf. ibid., 25–6 and 405–9.

13 Beardsley uses the term "interpretation" in a somewhat special sense, contrasting it with "description" and with "explication" and "elucidation." (See ibid., esp. 9–10 and 401.) However, my remarks remain equally valid if description (including explication) and elucidation are conceived of as being varieties of interpretation.

14 See the section "Interpretation in the 'Proper' Sense" in my "Five Kinds of Literary and Artistic Interpretation" below, esp. notes 37–8. Cf. also the essays by Torsten Pettersson and Göran Rossholm in this volume.

15 Hirsch, *Validity in Interpretation*, 8.

16 Ibid., 27, 31, et passim.

17 Ibid., 57.

18 Ibid., 57, 142–4, et passim.

19 Rorty, "The Pragmatist's Progress," 93.

20 Ibid., 106.

21 Ibid., 105.

22 See Jerrold Levinson, "Intention and Interpretation: A Last Look," in Gary Iseminger, ed., *Intention and Interpretation* (Philadelphia: Temple University Press, 1992), 221. It is worth emphasizing that I cannot here describe Levinson's standpoint in detail and so pass over several of its important particularities. To the best of my knowledge Levinson invented the now current designation of the position, but the first theorist to advocate this kind of analysis of the problem was William Tolhurst in his article "On What a Text Is and How It Means," *British Journal of Aesthetics* 19 (1979).

23 Jerrold Levinson, "Intention and Interpretation in Literature," in Levinson's *The Pleasures of Aesthetics: Philosophical Essays* (Ithaca and London: Cornell University Press, 1996), 175.

24 Ibid., 176–7.

25 Ibid., 177. In a later article by Levinson, the distinction between (normal) meaning and ludic meaning resurfaces as a distinction between the "*deter-*

minative" ("DM," "'does mean'") and the "*exploratory*" ("CM," "'could mean'") mode of interpretation. Jerrold Levinson,"Two Notions of Interpretation," in Arto Haapala and Ossi Naukkarinen, eds., *Interpretation and Its Boundaries* (Helsinki: Yliopistopaino/Helsinki University Press, 1999), 2.

26 Gary Iseminger, "An Intentional Demonstration?" in Iseminger, ed., *Intention and Interpretation*, 79.

27 Gary Iseminger, "Actual Intentionalism vs. Hypothetical Intentionalism," *Journal of Aesthetics and Art Criticism* 54 (1996): 319.

28 See, e.g., Erwin Leibfried, *Kritische Wissenschaft vom Text: Manipulation, Reflexion, transparente Poetologie*, 2nd ed. (Stuttgart: J.B. Metzlersche Verlagsbuchhandlung, 1972), 89 and 217 and John Reichert, *Making Sense of Literature* (Chicago: University of Chicago Press, 1977), 117–18.

29 See esp. Jeffrey Stout, "What Is the Meaning of a Text?" *New Literary History* 14 (1982). Rorty comes very close to Stout's position and also refers to Stout with approbation (Rorty, "The Pragmatist's Progress," 93, note 2).

30 Göran Hermerén, "Interpretation: Types and Criteria," in Joseph Margolis, ed., *The Worlds of Art and the World*, Grazer philosophische Studien, vol. 19 (Amsterdam: Rodopi, 1984), 133.

31 Ibid., 146–50.

32 Ibid., 160.

33 Ibid., 142–3.

34 Hermerén is aware of the problem but has no substantial solution to offer – cf. ibid., 155.

35 Richard Shusterman, *The Object of Literary Criticism* (Amsterdam: Rodopi; Würzburg: Königshausen und Neumann, 1984), 149.

36 Ibid., 168–9.

37 Annette Barnes, *On Interpretation: A Critical Analysis* (Oxford and New York: Basil Blackwell, 1988), 159.

38 Ibid., 160.

39 Ibid., 166.

40 As I see it, some types of what I call here "scholarly or critical investigations" will do that – and some types will not – but neither achievements of verbal or visual understanding nor appreciations will do so. See the discussion of some types of interpretation and their acceptability conditions in my "Five Kinds of Literary and Artistic Interpretation" below.

41 Patrick Colm Hogan, *On Interpretation: Meaning and Inference in Law, Psychoanalysis, and Literature* (Athens and London: University of Georgia Press, 1996); Robert Stecker, *Artworks: Definition Meaning Value* (University Park: Pennsylvania State University Press, 1997); Paul Thom, *Making Sense: A Theory of Interpretation* (Lanham: Rowman and Littlefield, 2000).

42 Hogan, *On Interpretation*, 11.

43 Ibid., esp. 12 and 92–3.

44 Ibid., esp. 12–26. The words quoted are taken from 13.

45 Ibid., 163.

46 Ibid.

47 Ibid., 176.

48 Stecker, *Artworks*, 6–7.

49 A time-honoured and in many cases reasonable way of understanding interpretations. Cf., e.g., Arnold Isenberg, "Critical Communication" (1949), esp. 147–50 and Charles L. Stevenson, "On the Reasons That Can Be Given for the Interpretation of a Poem," esp. 128–30, both in the first edition of Joseph Margolis, ed., *Philosophy Looks at the Arts: Contemporary Readings in Aesthetics* (New York: Charles Scribner's Sons, 1962).

50 In a later article, Stecker puts understanding on a par with appreciation as a motivation for interpretation: "When we interpret works of art and literature we are seeking to understand or to appreciate them, or to improve on our current level of understanding or appreciation. We do this by attempting to discover or, at least, ascribe on *some* basis, a meaning in or to the work in question, or to determine what significance the work has for us." Robert Stecker, "Interpretation," in Berys Gaut and Dominic McIver Lopes, eds.,*The Routledge Companion to Aesthetics* (London and New York: Routledge, 2001), 239.

51 Thom, *Making Sense*, 20.

52 Ibid., 106.

53 Cf. ibid., 54, 56, and 64 respectively.

54 Ibid., 63.

55 Ibid., 106.

56 Ibid., 54.

57 Cf. ibid. about kinds of representation.

58 Jorge J.E. Gracia, "Relativism and the Interpretation of Texts," in Joseph Margolis and Tom Rockmore, eds., *The Philosophy of Interpretation* (Oxford and Malden, Mass.: Blackwell, 1999). See, e.g., 46–7 and 59–60.

59 See, e.g., David Novitz, "Interpretation and Justification," 5, and Paul Thom, "On Changing the Subject," 73–4, both texts in Margolis and Rockmore, eds., *The Philosophy of Interpretation*.

60 Peter Lamarque, "Objects of Interpretation," in Margolis and Rockmore, eds., *The Philosophy of Interpretation*. Lamarque asks: "Does an interpretation bring to light a meaning (or some other aesthetic property) that is already part of the nature of the object, or does it in some way help constitute that nature?" (107). For literary works, the answer could natu-

rally be thought to differ depending on whether verbal understanding, or appreciation, or, for instance, the retrieval of authorial intention was at stake. However, Lamarque thinks that modes of interpretations and objects "are, in standard cases, deeply interlinked" (104) and keeps referring to literary interpretation, associated with literary works, as if it were a unified practice (see esp. 97, 104, 119).

61 Noël Carroll maintains, generally, that "interpretation is a matter of explaining why artworks have the features, including meanings, that they possess." See Noël Carroll, "Interpretation and Intention: The Debate between Hypothetical and Actual Intentionalism," in Margolis and Rockmore, eds., *The Philosophy of Interpretation*, 75. This cannot very well be true of what I have here called appreciations (nor, arguably, can it be true of many kinds of scholarly or critical interpretations).

62 Tom Rockmore says that textual interpretation can never be true: "I hold that interpretation cannot be true, although it can be false. An interpretation cannot be true since, except for special cases, which are probably very rare, almost any text admits of more than one reading." Tom Rockmore, "Interpretation as Historical, Constructivism, and History," in Margolis and Rockmore, eds., *The Philosophy of Interpretation*, 193.

I would argue that most types of textual interpretation are indeed neither true nor false, while there nevertheless exist some types that are (like retrievals of authorial intention; cf. my "Five Kinds of Literary and Artistic Interpretation" below).

63 Joseph Margolis, who contends that a bivalent logic is insufficient for the needs of the theory of interpretation, consistently speaks of the interpretation of literature and art as if it were all of one piece, and of literary and artistic meaning as if it were of one definite kind, not admitting of being located in the artist's or writer's mind. Joseph Margolis, "Relativism and Interpretive Objectivity," in Margolis and Rockmore, eds., *The Philosophy of Interpretation*, esp. 219 and 223.

Again, I would object that some types of interpretation of literature and art are in fact naturally seen as true or false (e.g., retrievals of intention), and some types of literary or artistic meaning (e.g., the author's or artist's intended meaning) are in fact locatable in the mind.

What Is an Interpretation?

Torsten Pettersson

The practice and nature of interpretation have called forth an impressive array of studies. They range from specialized treatments in the particularly prolific field of literary theory – exemplified by E.D. Hirsch's *Validity in Interpretation* (1967) and P.D. Juhl's *Interpretation* (1980) – through more diversified studies in anthologies such as *Interpretation and Overinterpretation* (1992) and *The Philosophy of Interpretation* (1999) to the magisterial philosophical synthesis of Joseph Margolis's *Interpretation Radical but Not Unruly* (1995).[1] But whatever their focus, insights, or differences, these discussions and numerous others have one thing in common: they fail to define their subject. Apparently the concept of interpretation is so ingrained in our culture that even scholars who devote considerable energy to a scrutiny of some of its aspects see no need to define or delimit the concept itself beyond a few simple assumptions. These often remain implicit, and the occasional articulations of them have not been very illuminating: Monroe Beardsley, for instance, defines "a critical interpretation" as "a statement that purports to declare the 'meaning' of a work of art," and Paul Thom states that an interpretation is "a view of an object that purports to make sense of it by representing it in a particular way."[2]

In what follows I will attempt to remedy this deficiency in discussions of interpretation by formulating and answering two questions: What is considered to be an interpretation in Western culture in our time? What types of interpretation can be usefully distinguished and what are their characteristics? As the first question suggests, I presuppose no transhistorical essence of interpretation; but I do assume that beneath the multiplicity of language games in which interpretation occurs, there is, at a given point in time, a shared understanding of the concept which is worth exploring.

The field to be thus organized is a very extensive one, as is suggested by Göran Hermerén's list of some uses of the term "interpretation": emendation, linguistic interpretation, interpretation of the author's meaning, interpretation of intentions, psychological extrapolation, application, theoretical reinterpretation, interpretation of symptoms, historical reconstruction, augmentation of value, and performance.[3] What is required, however, for a satisfactory coverage of the field is not a haphazard list but, first, a definition of essential features: what are the criteria that must be fulfilled if an entity is to be regarded as an interpretation? Second, if different types of interpretation need to be distinguished, both their common features and their divergences must be made clear.

Furthermore, a project of this kind must strike a balance between unadulterated description and pure stipulation. Merely to amalgamate everything that is sometimes called interpretation would lead to a formless and watered-down concept of little interest. A core of meaning has to be distilled from usage, but on the other hand the occasional stipulation that makes this possible can extend only to relatively borderline cases and must leave untouched the instances of interpretation that many observers would regard as central and paradigmatic. Anything else would be an exercise in wilful eccentricity.

No doubt these requirements can be met and divisions and subdivisions made in various ways – there is no one way of organizing the field. Since my aim is to bring out the underlying logic of our current conception of interpretation, I wish to keep divisions to a minimum. This has resulted in the differentiation of three types of interpretation. I shall present them in the form of a step-by-step delimitation of one type coupled with indications of how and why the other two types can be usefully distinguished from it.

It follows from the requirement of reasonable descriptive accuracy that, rather than trying to present a new and surprising slant on interpretation, I wish to tease out all the elements that make up a concept of interpretation that is well established and familiar but insufficiently articulated. I can therefore, without anticipating too much of the argument, summarize my main points in advance to facilitate the reader's passage through this essay:

> An interpretation I_1 is a wittingly produced coherent conceptual representation of the activities or products of sentient beings. It focuses on elements which the interpreter takes to be poorly understood by the addressee and attempts to clarify their meaning or function.

The substance of my discussion will consist in motivating each of these elements and delimiting them from other cultural practices that are similar but do not in fact constitute interpretation, or constitute interpretation of the two other kinds, I_2 and I_3 (defined at the end of this paper).

I wish to emphasize the fact that the following discussion is integral to the above delimitation of the concept, which should not be regarded as a definition in the strictest sense of a self-contained and self-explanatory set of conditions. Instead, this essay as a whole provides an extended definition of the concept of interpretation. Within that framework, each of the elements in the above condensed statement, which may look vague or ambiguous on its own, will derive a full and more precise meaning from a particularized consideration of a wide range of examples.

Even so, one may wonder if this kind of delimitation is appropriate. Should it not be replaced by a looser enumeration of characteristics of interpretation allowing for a number of borderline cases and a discussion in terms of sliding scales rather than definite properties which enforce in-or-out decisions? The answer, I believe, is that such a procedure would certainly be more manageable, but also less rewarding. The point of being forced to come down on one side of the fence is partly to provide what I take to be the most defensible delimitation of the concept of interpretation. But the point is also, in cases where some readers disagree, to provoke them into an awareness of their own implicit assumptions about interpretation. In discussing my ideas with colleagues in the aesthetic disciplines, philosophy and semiotics, I have discovered a disturbing consequence of the prevalent neglect of the question of definition: no two people seem to have the same conception of exactly what range of examples is covered by the concept of interpretation. This rarely emerges in other kinds of aesthetic or philosophical debates because they generally deal with obvious core examples of interpretation. But a definition of the kind that I am attempting reveals the disagreement which usually remains hidden but which may contribute to the inconclusive dissent or frustrating deadlock that characterizes many debates about interpretation. If, unbeknownst to themselves, interlocutors A, B, and C think of partially different sets of examples when they say "interpretation," is it not likely that this is one reason why they fail to reach agreement, or even fruitfully defined dissent, in their arguments over whether interpretations decode or project, are normative or descriptive, can or cannot be true or false, or are best described in intentionalist or conventionalist terms? One central aim of this paper is to provoke an awareness of this problem by means of the following definatory discussion.

1. *An interpretation I_1 is a wittingly produced coherent conceptual representation ...*

An interpretation is on the one hand something like Cleanth Brooks's reading of a poem, Monroe Beardsley's explanation of Aristotle's concept of catharsis, or Gibbon's exposition of the fall of the Roman Empire. On the other hand it is something like von Karajan's rendering of a Mahler symphony, Richter's performance of a Beethoven piano sonata, Sir Laurence Olivier's embodiment of Hamlet, Sir Peter Brook's production of a Shakespeare play, or Béjart's ballet version of Wagner's *Ring* cycle. A possible view of the relationship between the two types would be that it is one of mere homonymy, and that the latter, performative type need not be considered in conjunction with the former. This, however, strikes me as being too extreme because there appear to be substantial links between the two types.

First, the fact that they are both habitually referred to as "interpretations" must not be dismissed lightly. Even though we need not assume a one-to-one correspondence between linguistic usage and conceptual structure, usage is an important clue to the prevailing conceptualization. Second, discursive and performative interpretations are linked by the fact that they both constitute attempts to present in a certain way an object that can also be presented in other ways. Third, we can sometimes see obvious points of contact between these two different kinds of presentation. Thus musicologists may write interpretations of Beethoven's Appassionata Sonata as either an essentially (proto-)Romantic or a classicist work, but the same basic points can be made by playing the sonata in a certain way: Sviatoslav Richter's explosive performance gives us a Romantic Appassionata, while Murray Perrahia's more delicate reading emphasizes its classicist character.[4] Finally, as Göran Rossholm's contribution to this volume indicates, there are similarities between some (though not all) of the theoretical questions evoked by the two types of interpretation.

Performative interpretation thus legitimately belongs to the field that we are surveying, but it shows sufficient peculiarities of its own to be distinguished as a special type I_3. It is, for one thing, sensuously presentational rather than discursive or conceptual. Often partly or wholly non-verbal, it relies on staging, choreography, body language, musical means of expression, and so on. Even when it is verbal – like Charles Nordhoff and James N. Hall's novel *Mutiny on the Bounty* viewed as an interpretation of a historical event – it is not primarily conceptual (reasoned, argumentative). Instead, it resorts to other means of expression such as the elaboration of character traits, ulterior motives, dialogue, and subsidiary events – all of which may be unattested in any extant source.

Second, a performative interpretation usually constitutes a work of art in its own right[5] and is therefore allowed to be less obviously subservient to its object than is a discursive interpretation. The latter, as it is usually understood, is expected to illuminate its object and not to make statements that are obviously contravened by it. In contrast, musicians may be respected for their personal vision even when the tempo of their performance clearly flouts the composer's indications; or the director of a play may depart radically from the writer's stage directions and find acceptance for this if the result is considered rewarding enough.

To return to the main line of definition, a conceptual kind of interpretation seeks rational organization and clarity rather than the sensuous concreteness of its artistic counterpart. It usually achieves its aim verbally, as a discussion presented in a book, article, review, lecture, or the like. But since its ultimate objective is conceptualization, rather than linguistic articulation as such, it may also be communicated in such forms as sign language, formulas, charts, or diagrams. Thus a map of Jupiter may be regarded as an interpretation of the available empirical data (where a sensuous presentation of sorts is incidental and subservient to conceptualization).

But whatever its mode of communication, it would seem that the presentation must be reasonably coherent to count as an interpretation. Consider the following example:

(i) Hamlet is a coward. Ophelia is not really mad. Hamlet's mother is evil.

This, I would contend, is not an interpretation of *Hamlet*. It is a sequence of three separate and partial minuscule interpretations, which would have to be related to each other by a coherent argument if they were to emerge as a (more comprehensive) interpretation of the play.

Furthermore, in order to constitute an interpretation, the coherent conceptual representation must have been produced wittingly. This means, for one thing, that it must not be accidental. Imagine that I have seen a film in which the male protagonist joins the French Foreign Legion for reasons that I cannot understand. Leaving the theatre, I hear the following comment in the street: "He felt his life was over when his girlfriend left him." Taking this to be the observation of another film-goer, I could regard it as a plausible interpretation of the character's motivation. But if the originator of the comment was a passer-by who had not seen the film and was referring to a friend of his, his observation clearly would not be an interpretation of the film; the accidental correspondence between the statement and the film would not suffice to make the statement an interpretation. Second, even an intended correspondence does not suffice unless it is based on a reasonable knowledge of the object. Let us assume that I have slept through the film in its entirety, and leaving the theatre I am asked by a friend why I thought the protagonist joined the Foreign Legion. Too embarrassed to admit my somnolence, I hazard a shot in the dark: "He felt his life was over when his girlfriend left him." Even if this was germane to the film, it would not strictly speaking be an interpretation because it is not based on even a minimal knowledge of the object. For an interpretation to be produced wittingly, then, means that it is neither accidentally applicable to the object nor a random lucky guess.

2. An interpretation I_1 is a wittingly produced coherent conceptual representation *of* ...

An interpretation is always related to an object, *of* which it is an interpretation. That relation may be implicit, but we can never say "That is an interesting interpretation" *tout court*, without a shared understanding of what object the interpretation refers to. Where no such understanding, explicit or implicit, is available, we are dealing, not with an interpretation, but with an expression of opinion or subjective experience, philosophical reflection, speculation, or the like. However, in assessing whether or not the relation exists, we show great tolerance because it is the nature of interpretations to highlight only a selection of features, and often in a surprising manner. Take the following statements made about Picasso's *Guernica:*

(ii) It is an indictment of the suffering and chaos brought about by war.
(iii) It is a revelation of the suffering inflicted on innocent animals like the horse and the bull by human ruthlessness.
(iv) It is a celebration of the multifarious, bustling exuberance of life.
(v) It is an imaginative rendering of the spots that often form on the skin of a ripe banana.
(vi) It is an expression of the difficulty of learning to type.

The first three of these, I would argue, are interpretations. (iii) may be idiosyncratically selective and (iv) clearly erroneous, but, along with the more normal (ii), they maintain a recognizable link with such observable features of Picasso's painting as the animal heads and the throng of people and animals. (v) and (vi) present themselves as interpretations, and on some very wide understanding of the concept could perhaps be accepted as such despite being so outlandish. However, I consider their links to their alleged object to be so tenuously artificial or non-existent that – if they are not presented as jokes or parodies of over-sophisticated interpretations – (v) and (vi) are best regarded as hallucinatory projections masquerading as interpretations.[6]

The referential link between an interpretation and its object may seem to be a self-evident fact, and it is certainly relied upon in all fields as a standard of accuracy in attempts to refute misguided interpretations. Thus in our example, we could challenge (iv) by pointing out that the facial expressions portrayed by Picasso reflect suffering rather than joy so clearly that the painting cannot be seen as a celebration of life's exuberance. Nevertheless, the whole existence of the referential link has been contested by some theorists of literary interpretation. The most prominent of them is Stanley Fish, whose position remains the paradigmatic example of constructivism in literary theory. Fish, as is well known, claims that "Interpreters do not decode poems; they make them" in accordance with the conventions of the interpretive community to which they belong. There may be substantial agreement among them, but this, "rather than being a proof of the stability of objects, is a testimony to the power of an interpretive community to constitute the objects." There is, Fish argues, "no core of agreement *in* the text," only some agreement concerning "the way of *producing* the text."[7]

Fish, then, denies the existence of an independent object of literary interpretation and hence denies the existence of a referential link between the two. But his claim that the interpretive strategies – and not to any extent the properties of the object – are the exclusive source of meaning and acceptability is clearly wrong. If it was correct, and generally accepted possible meanings of words in the text (independent of any interpretation) counted for nothing, any established strategy should be applicable to any literary work. One should be able to argue that the protagonist of *Othello* is prevented from enacting his desire for revenge by an incestuous infatuation with his mother and a consequent identification with his uncle. This is certainly an accepted strategy, applicable to *Hamlet.* So that if the source of the "mechanisms for ruling out readings ... is not the text but the presently recognized interpretive strategies for producing the text," as Fish puts it (347), why cannot this strategy be applied to *Othello* as well as to *Hamlet*?

Fish does not confront the objection in precisely this form, but he does discuss a similar example suggested by Norman Holland: Why is it unacceptable, within the framework of the present literary community, to interpret Faulkner's "A Rose for Emily" as being about Inuit? The reason, Fish maintains, is that "there is at present no interpretive strategy for producing" the story "that would result in the emergence of obviously Eskimo meanings" (346). He then goes on to explain that such an interpretation might become possible if it was revealed that Faulkner always believed himself to be an Inuit changeling, and if critics elaborated a symbolic or allusive system showing the presence of this newly discovered "fact." Here Fish curiously shifts his ground. The concept of an interpretive strategy no longer designates the large-scale assumptions which govern our interpretations by allowing certain types (such as "nature vs culture") and disallowing others (such as spiritistic messages). Instead the concept has turned into the equivalent of an acceptable interpretation of an individual work (an Inuit reading of Faulkner's story) and the conditions for its acceptability (Faulkner's belief that he was an Inuit). When confronted with awkward evidence Fish has thus been forced to abandon his meaningful, though misguided, claim that our reading is wholly governed by institutional conventions fashioning the text in their image. He cannot maintain, as he should be able to in order to support his theory, that the Inuit reading is even now acceptable since elaborate allusive systems are accepted interpretive strategies (for instance in interpretations of Blake and Yeats), and since the text of the story itself, in Fish's view, can offer no resistance. Fish's claim has in fact become a circular one: an interpretation is acceptable if it can be produced by a recognized interpretive strategy, but that strategy includes all the considerations which in each individual case make the interpretation acceptable. Thus Fish is unable to prove that correspondence with the text (as an entity independent of the interpretation) is not one of these considerations.

A further counter-argument can be stated more briefly. As I have already suggested, it is possible to persuade a person to abandon his or her interpretation by pointing to parts or aspects of the work which it cannot accommodate. This empirical fact is in itself awkward for champions of the view that the work is wholly constituted by the interpretation since argumentative reference "past" the interpretation to the work should not be possible. The proponents of this view will, of course, reply that in such cases the interpretation is not challenged by reference to the work, but by another set of principles for producing the work, as Fish claims (353); and that the disagreement is thus a "metacritical" one about the validity and elaboration of the approaches themselves.[8] But this defence breaks down on two counts. First, as we have seen, the reason why a certain interpretive strategy is acceptable with regard to one Shakespeare play but not to another is not metacritical. It concerns, not the strategy as such, but the relevance of its application. Because of qualities which must be independent of the interpretation (since it remains constant), one text responds satisfactorily to a given strategy, and another does not. Second, it would seem that we can invalidate an interpretation with reference to the text even without providing an alternative interpretation in any reasonably strong sense of the word. We can simply point out that none of the meanings which certain words in the text may conceivably have according to native speakers of the language "fit" the interpretation, and admit that these words pose a problem which we are also unable to solve. In so doing we have referred to the text without substituting an alternative interpretation "presiding over its production," in Fish's words (354): we have been unable to "produce" the text (i.e., understand it in certain way) at all.

These facts – the limitations imposed by the work on the application of an interpretive strategy that is acceptable in itself, and the possibility of referring to the work even without providing an interpretation of it – can only be explained on the assumption that, at least in some aspects, the work exists independently of the interpretation as an entity with which the interpretation corresponds or seeks to correspond. An interpretation, to repeat, is always an interpretation *of* something.

This means that the success of an interpretation depends in part on the characteristics of the object. It does not follow, however, that a simple correspondence model of this activity is thereby validated. Clearly, interpretation is a much more complicated process involving at least selection, distribution of emphases, and combinatory creativity. While pure constructivism is misguided, the field therefore remains open to many different construals of that process. They may for instance range, along one relevant scale, from the standpoint that "truth" must remain some kind of regulatory ideal for interpretive statements to conceptions couched in the logically weaker terms of plausibility or acceptability. The minimum requirement for a viable account is only that it preserves a modicum of contact between interpretations and their objects.

The second point that needs to be clarified concerns the relation to another relevant dimension of reflection: the dispute between conventionalists and intentionalists which surfaces in Anders Pettersson's introduction to the present volume. It might be thought that the former are favoured by my emphasis on the necessary connections between a conceptual interpretation and its object, as their models of interpretation concentrate on that connection and exclude consideration of underlying intentions. However, there is in fact no such bias in my account because intentionalists may reconcile the importance which it accords to that connection with their preferences in one of three ways. They may either preserve a degree of respect for the object (such as a work of art), but add to it contextual considerations suggesting authorial intentions; or they may say that in an account as general as mine nothing prevents them from regarding those intentions (rather than their various manifestations) as the object with which the interpretation is connected. Finally, they may see no problem in the connection that I have emphasized, but insist that the object is in itself fundamentally constituted by intentionality.

3. An interpretation I_1 is a wittingly produced coherent conceptual representation of *the activities or products of sentient beings* ...

If, when considering a painting of a landscape surmounted by a blue sky, I find that a cloud looks like a sailboat, I may say that I interpret it as (a representation of) a sailboat; and I may go on to comment on how it symbolizes a longing for freedom, open expanses of sea, departure from the enclosed landscape, and so on. If, on the other hand, I see a real cloud with a similar appearance, I might say that it has the shape or semblance of a sailboat, that it looks like or reminds me of a sailboat, but not that I interpret it as a sailboat. Analogously, I may interpret a painting of a fire as showing people dancing, but a real fire I can only "see," not "interpret," as a group of dancers. The reason for this difference would seem to be that I know that the paintings are created by artists, whereas the cloud and the fire are fortuitous natural formations. Consequently, if I change my understanding of the latter I may also alter the categorization of my impressions. Viewing nature, not as a set of physical phenomena, but as the book of God, I might well say that I "interpret" the cloud as a sailboat, and go on to consider what God wishes to communicate to me. Or, given reasons to believe that someone had rigged the fire to produce certain formations, I could be said to "interpret"them as a group of dancers. What matters is the assumption that the object of my attention originates in someone's activity rather than mere physical processes.

As the example indicates, the sentient origin that allows the concept of interpretation I_1 to apply may be human or superhuman (God, gods, demons, the spirits of the deceased), but it may also be lodged in animals: I interpret the dog's behaviour as a desire to be taken out, and zoologists interpret certain movements of bees as a method for signalling the whereabouts of new supplies of nectar. Exactly how far into the realm of the invertebrates we are willing to extend the application of the concept is to some extent an open question depending on our view of the relevant animals. If we consider an amoeba to be a sentient being, we may interpret its movements as a quest for light, whereas if we regard them as wholly automatic cellular reactions, the concept would not apply. But whatever our decision, we apparently preserve the conceptual link between the process we call interpretation and the assumption that its objects originate in some kind of mind.

At this point it would be convenient to invoke Dilthey's distinction between *Verstehen* and *Erklären* and maintain that interpretation pertains only to the former, human (or more generally "mental") realm. But in fact that is not the case, for geologists may well be said to interpret a mineral layer as an indication of a prehistoric volcanic eruption; astronomers interpret the curvature of light in outer space as a manifestation of a black hole; and I may interpret the cloud as a portent of rain. In these cases, clearly, there is no assumption of sentient origin. Instead, we trace causal chains backward in time (from mineral to volcanic activity, or from curved light to the gravity that caused and keeps causing it); and we make a *pars pro toto* judgment followed by an extrapolation to a consequence in the future (the cloud is the most visible part of atmospheric conditions that will cause rain). To put it in general terms, in this kind of interpretation we attempt to chart the spatial, temporal, and/or causal ramifications of physical phenomena according to the natural laws we believe to be valid. This should be demarcated as a separate type of interpretation I_2, distinguishable from the first type, which is focused on the activities and products of sentient beings.

The difference in focus is reflected in the kind of reasoning available to us. When dealing with sentient (usually human) beings, we realize that the regularities in their behaviour, which our interpretation to some extent relies on, are at best partial and conditional because the workings of a mind are always variable and never fully transparent. This makes for fluidity, wide margins of error, and, frequently, a lack of final confirmation even in principle. In contrast, when interpreting physical processes, we may assume the absolute validity of the laws of physics and chemistry: certain atmospheric conditions will always produce rain, and a certain mineral can only be of volcanic origin. The main interpretive question is one of categorization: is this really the kind of cloud that goes together with these atmospheric conditions, is this really an exclusively volcanic kind of mineral? But once categorization has been settled, causal, spatial, and temporal connections can be pursued with confidence – given that all variables are under control – because those connections are assumed to follow the unconditional laws of nature. This is one essential difference which motivates the distinction between interpretation I_1 and interpretation I_2, both of which are conceptual rather than performative.

It should be noted, however, that this separation of the two does not entail that sentient beings or their artifacts can never be subjected to interpretation I_2. They can – because both they and their artifacts are necessarily part of the physical world and may temporarily be considered only from that perspective. Thus a doctor, interpreting a fever and a rash of a given description as the consequences of a certain kind of infection, views the patient, not as a person with a unique and partly unpredictable personality, but as a physiological organism that reacts in a predictable way to a well-known disease. The problem is merely one of categorization: is this really that kind of rash? Or to take another example, this time of artifacts, I may interpret a strange noise from the engine of my car as an indication that the fuel pump is giving out because of the long years of service that will inevitably have caused it to wear out. In such cases – unlike those of "pure" physical phenomena – it is often possible to switch to interpretation I_1 (and go on to say that the infection resulted from the patient's recklessness, or the malfunction of the pump from the manufacturer's use of cheap materials). But the initial step is an instance of interpretation I_2.

Before returning to the definition of interpretation I_1, it is worth noting that where human beings are concerned it is not always clear which of the two types is applicable, and the selection of one or the other may have considerable consequences. If viewed as a sentient being (endowed with will and intentions), a person is responsible for his or her actions. On the other hand, if he or she is regarded as an organism, in which a certain medical condition produces a certain type of behaviour, he or she is not. In some legal cases the choice between I_1 and I_2 may thus be tantamount to the difference between conviction and severe punishment on the one hand and acquittal or a reduced sentence on the other.

4. An interpretation I_1 is a wittingly produced coherent conceptual representation of the activities or products of sentient beings. *It focuses on elements which the interpreter takes to be poorly understoodby the addressee ...*

An interpretation often contains some background information about the object and its place in a wider context, and it may contain an evaluation of the object. But in order to remain an interpretation it must focus on the elements that seem to stand in need of clarification.[9] However, what is poorly understood depends on the level of knowledge and sophistication attained by the intended addressee of the interpretation. In what may be termed "spearhead interpretation," presented as a novel contribution to specialists in a field, the assumption is that the elements focused on are puzzling in the absolute sense of never having been properly understood by anyone. In many other cases of what may be called "initiatory interpretation," the elements in question are not puzzling in this absolute sense, but need to be explained to non-specialists. At a conference of Renaissance scholars it may, for instance, be regarded as an obvious fact that "A little more than kin, and less than kind" (*Hamlet* 1.2.65) means "A little more than an ordinary kinsman but less than a kindly son," but a high school teacher explaining this to his students nevertheless provides an interpretation of the passage. And this clearly remains true even if, unaware that a colleague has already gone over the passage with the students in question, the teacher is mistaken in assuming a need for clarification. On the other hand, it can be argued that if he makes no such assumption and knowingly produces a gratuitous explanation, it is not a genuine interpretation, but something like a parody or a test of the students' reactions.

As a further example of this distinction, imagine a school corridor where a stylized sign prohibits running indoors. In the course of introducing a new student to the school, a teacher takes him to the sign and explains its not altogether transparent meaning. This is an interpretation. On the other hand, the teacher may also catch one of the other students running in the corridor. He takes him to the sign and explains its meaning in painstaking detail. Since this student knows what the sign means, and the teacher knows that he knows it, this is not an interpretation; it is an exercise in discipline and sarcastic humiliation which merely assumes the trappings of an interpretation.

The assumption of insufficient understanding on the part of the addressee can take two forms in both initiatory and spearhead interpretation. Its starting-point may be the fact that something is manifestly perplexing, like the above quotation from *Hamlet*. But it may also call attention to problems and hidden meanings in what seems to be transparent. Thus Hamlet's statement, two lines after the phrase just quoted, that he is unwell because he is "too much i' the sun" is not obviously problematic. But the interpretation of a good teacher would add the further meaning that Hamlet is too much "in the (relation of) son" (i.e., the son of his uncle through his mother's marriage to him, as well as the son of his biological father). Analogously, scholars addressing their peers may turn to well-known problems such as the reasons for Hamlet's procrastination or the possible occurrence of ghosts in Henry James's *The Turn of the Screw;* but more often than not, they may detect new problems and proceed to provide an interpretation, as when feminists took up the dormant question of the portrayal of female characters in novels by male writers.

As all this suggests, I would argue that the addressee is an essential, implicit element in the concept of interpretation, as is the recognizable link to the object of interpretation. However, this does not mean that an interpretation must always be publicly formulated. If I do not understand why a character in a film that I have just seen commits suicide, I may go over the film in my mind and piece together a satisfactory explanation for his decision. That is surely an interpretation even if I do not communicate it to anyone. The "addressee," in this case, would be myself, or that part of me that was first perplexed and then enlightened by my powers of ratiocination. It is fair to say that we produce "private" interpretations of this kind almost every day in our encounters with friends, strangers, political events, artworks – the entire social world around us. The test of whether they really are coherent conceptual representations of their objects is our ability to communicate them if necessary. If someone asks me about the suicide in the film and I can provide an explanation immediately, what I had in my mind was an interpretation; if I cannot, it was merely a set of inchoate observations.

5. An interpretation I_1 is a wittingly produced coherent conceptual representation of the activities or products of sentient beings. It focuses on elements which the interpreter takes to be poorly understood by the addressee *and attempts to clarify their meaning or function.*

Imagine three texts about the German poet Paul Celan (1920–70). After ample exemplification of the problems of understanding posed by his hermetic poetry, they continue, respectively, in a vein that can be summarized as follows:

(vii) Celan concocts a random jumble of words that communicates nothing of human significance and is best dismissed as humbug.
(viii) Celan refreshingly places us in contact with all that is mysterious in our existence and allows us to transcend the boundaries of stultifying rationality.

(ix) The key to resolving Celan's paradoxes lies in their relation to the Holocaust, whose mangling of human souls and bodies it depicts in fragmented symbols.

As in the above case of *Guernica,* these could all be seen as interpretations in a loose sense. However, it seems to me that the aim of clarification is such an important core element in the prevalent understanding of interpretation that a less all-embracing conception is more apposite. I would therefore suggest that (vii) and (viii) may possibly be termed interpretations of Celan's intentions, but in relation to the texts of the poems they are not interpretations because they merely point to and evaluate the difficulties of understanding. Although all three focus on puzzling elements in their object, only (ix), which also seeks to resolve the puzzlement, can usefully be termed an interpretation.

The attempt to clarify meaning thus forms part of the definition of interpretation. I should emphasize, however, that the mere attempt may be sufficient for an entity to meet the definition. Flawed, misguided, obviously incorrect interpretations are still interpretations, as long as they retain a recognizable link to their object and make an effort to clarify elements that are assumed to be poorly understood.

The focus of the attempt at clarification is often on elements that are the bearers of meaning in a very wide sense. We interpret the meaning of words or artworks, the import of political events, the meaning – intended or otherwise – of a friend's absence from our birthday party, or the true purport of the speeches made at the party. This is the kind of interpretation that discussions of the concept primarily deal with, and mostly to the exclusion of other types. However, it is clear that even when we address the activities or products of a sentient being within the confines of interpretation I_1, what we interpret is not always meaning. For instance, when I puzzle over a particularly perplexing constituent in an assembly kit, I would more naturally be said to be attempting an interpretation of its "function": its place and mode of operation in relation to other parts. This is a focus of interpretation that occurs in our dealings with artworks alongside the interpretation of meaning (as in the interpretive statement that the function of the porter in *Macbeth* is to provide comic relief). In our confrontation with human artifacts that are not works of art, this is often the dominant, and sometimes the only possible focus of interpretation: tools, instruments, and utensils usually do not have meaning, but they do have functions that are frequently the object of interpretation. However, this may also be true of human behaviour, particularly when it is viewed as part of a concerted action. Thus in observing a player in a football match I hardly interpret the "meaning" of his movements, but I do interpret their "function" in a larger configuration of players devised by their coach.

A final problem connected with points 4 and 5 above is the relation between interpreting and knowing. This is the demarcation line of the concept of interpretation that has been most adequately treated in the past. With some nuances of specification, considerable agreement has been reached that we can interpret only that which is not obvious; what is transparently knowable cannot be interpreted, only "described."[10] We are not interpreting when we observe that the sky is blue, that the *New York Times* is written in English, or that the cutlery next to our plates is for eating with. There is a complication here because almost anything may be poorly understood by, and hence be interpretable for, such addressees as children and people with mental or perceptual deficiencies. But in the community of "normal" adults consensus obtains in many matters, and where it does the concept of interpretation is not applicable.

The problem that remains, however, is that the process of clarification can sometimes produce such insights that what was at first poorly understood in the end seems obvious and transparently knowable. This is not so much true of our attempts to establish the meaning of artworks, political events, or human behaviour. In such cases we realize that alternative specifications are always possible and indisputable knowledge unattainable: even well-founded insights remain interpretations. But the interpretation of the function of artifacts sometimes results in full certainty. An oddly shaped hook in a hotel bathroom prompts interpretation, but when I have understood its function and tested it to my full satisfaction, what is the status of the statement: "This is a bottle-opener"? On the one hand, one would like to say that, despite the initial puzzlement of an inexperienced hotel guest, that function is as obvious as the function of cutlery, and will readily be confirmed by all seasoned travellers. The statement would then be a description, not an interpretation. On the other hand, it may seem odd to call the result of a process of interpretation something other than an interpretation.

This is clearly a gray area where both solutions can be justified. I prefer the former because it emphasizes the communal point of view on which my scrutiny of interpretation has been based: what is generally held to be obvious emerges as a description even when it has to be interpreted by or for some individuals. Moreover, the change in specification, once confidence has been attained, from "(the result of) an interpretation" to "a description" is in fact not so much a logical oddity as a reflection of an ongoing social practice. Almost everything that we consider obvious – from the applicability of the most common words to the use of simple tools and appliances – has at one time in our lives been interpreted for us by others or by ourselves. But when the relevant insights have been reached and have become well established, they pass into our repository of evident knowledge. They change their status, as it were, from more or less laboriously accomplished interpretations to effortless descriptions, and the process is repeated whenever we are introduced to the basics of new activities like bridge or golf or the acquisition of a foreign language. If we were to insist that the result of an interpretation is always an interpretation – and not a description, even when it is indisputably accurate – we would in fact be forced to all but abolish the concept of description, since all members of the group that agrees on what is obvious have at some point in their lives acquired their knowledge through interpretation. I therefore conclude that a statement of what is considered indisputable by a relevant community is a description, regardless of its origin in interpretation and of the continuing need for initiatory interpretation.[11]

Of course, communities make mistakes, so that what was once considered a description of an indisputable fact – such as the earth being flat – later turns out to have been a (misguided) interpretation. In such cases the specification must indeed be changed, and we must concede that, by the same token, observations that we now consider incontrovertible may be proved wrong. However, this must not lead us to conclude that all statements are interpretations because there is no guarantee that they may not, at some point in time, be impugned. What we are concerned with is not timeless truth, but conventions and conceptions obtaining in a given society at a given time. And they definitely comprise a distinction between that which is considered obvious and that which is subject to interpretation.

To sum up, we have found that the practice of interpretation can be divided into three types defined as follows:

> An interpretation I_1 is a wittingly produced coherent conceptual representation of the activities or products of sentient beings. It focuses on elements which the interpreter takes to be poorly understood by the addressee and attempts to clarify their meaning or function.

> An interpretation I_2 is a wittingly produced coherent conceptual representation of processes and states of affairs in the physical world. It focuses on elements which the interpreter takes to be poorly understood by the addressee and attempts to clarify their spatial, temporal, and/or causal relations.

> An interpretation I_3 is a wittingly produced coherent and sensuously presentational representation of an artwork or an aspect of reality.

Of the three types, the first is the implicit or explicit topic of most discussions of the concept of interpretation as it is encountered in the arts or more widely in society. It has therefore also received most of my attention, and as a result the definitions of I_2 and I_3 must be offered somewhat more tentatively than that of I_1.

A NOTE ON THE INTERPRETATION OF ART

The general characteristics of I_1 having been determined, it might seem a natural move to establish a subdivision between interpretations of art and interpretations of other human phenomena. With what degree of vigour that distinction should be made is very much a moot point. It is clear that there are both analogies and differences between aesthetic and non-aesthetic interpretation, but there is considerable disagreement concerning their respective proportions and much to be said on both sides. Analogists emphasize that art is produced by someone as a kind of "message" addressed to others and comprehendable in terms of shared conventions. It is a form of communication which may follow some special conventions of its own, but which does not, in its fundamental principles, differ from other forms of communication. Hence, there is no essential difference between the interpretation of art and other forms of interpretation in the human realm. Differentialists, on the other hand, maintain that such observable similarities are superficial. In a more profound sense, they insist, art is not a form of communication because its aim usually is not to convey information and opinions or to influence the actions of the addressee. It may do so in some special cases such as the *roman à thèse*, but its central and dominant characteristic is that it presents verbal, visual, or acoustic configurations for us to enjoy for their own sake and reflect on in a "disinterested" manner that is far removed from our attitude to other human activities or products. Furthermore, all the elements of the artwork and the conventions which it draws on are geared to this special purpose. Therefore, on this view, the interpretation of art has a very particular character which subsumes and modifies the application of non-aesthetic skills (such as the understanding of human behaviour which we bring to our interpretation of fictional characters).[12]

As this suggests, the question of the specificity of aesthetic interpretation is connected with problems concerning the definition of art and the relationship between art and reality. Since they are notoriously intractable, it is not surprising that it is impossible to furnish an answer to the question that would be clear and comprehensive without being tendentious. Determinations will have to be made in different ways for different kinds of artworks and interpretations. A possible starting-point for that enterprise is provided by the essays in this volume, which, from a variety of vantage points, differentiate between types of interpretation.

NOTES

1 See E.D. Hirsch, Jr, *Validity in Interpretation* (New Haven: Yale University Press, 1967); P.D. Juhl, *Interpretation: An Essay in the Philosophy of Literary Criticism* (Princeton, New Jersey: Princeton University Press, 1980); Umberto Eco et al., *Interpretation and Overinterpretation*, ed. Stefan Collini (Cambridge: Cambridge University Press, 1992); Joseph Margolis and Tom Rockmore, eds., *The Philosophy of Interpretation* (Oxford: Blackwell, 1999); and Joseph Margolis, *Interpretation Radical but Not Unruly: The New Puzzle of the Arts and History* (Berkeley and Los Angeles: University of California Press, 1995).

2 Monroe C. Beardsley, *Aesthetics: Problems in the Philosophy of Criticism*, 2nd ed. (Indianapolis: Wayne State University Press, 1980), 9, and Paul Thom, *Making Sense: A Theory of Interpretation* (Lanham: Rowman and Littlefield, 2000), 20.

The rule of non-definition also obtains, alas, in Torsten Pettersson, *Literary Interpretation: Current Models and a New Departure* (Åbo: Åbo Academy Press, 1988). To my knowledge, the nearest thing to an exception to the rule is supplied by Annette Barnes, *On Interpretation: A Critical Analysis* (Oxford: Basil Blackwell, 1988). She offers no full definition of interpretation, but in delimiting the concept from that of description, she gradually assembles a list of characteristics (detailed on p. 154), which may be regarded as a partial definition. It is in the main comparable to point 4 in my definition.

3 Göran Hermerén, "Interpretation: Types and Criteria," in Joseph Margolis, ed., *The Worlds of Art and the World*, Grazer philosophische Studien 19 (Amsterdam: Rodopi, 1984), 131–69. The list of types of interpretation appears on pp. 146–50.

4 Richter's reading is on the RCA disc 07863 56518 2, Perrahia's on the Sony disc MK 39344.

5 Performative interpretations are for the most part artworks, but one can think of special cases where they are not. If a high school student has committed suicide, a commission inquiring into the causes might encounter a pantomime where students enact a classroom situation: a stern teacher treats his students dismissively and contemptuously, they cringe and look depressed, and one of them withdraws into a corner where he makes the gesture that signifies cutting one's throat. This would hardly be an artwork, but it would be a performative interpretation presented by the students of why, in their view, their friend killed himself. Because such special cases are possible, my definition of interpretation I_3 will not include the element of artistic purpose even though it is present in the vast majority of performative interpretations.

6 Anders Pettersson has pointed out to me that something like (v) could be presented as an explication of a special code. In my view, however, this would constitute, not an act of interpretation, but one of mechanical decoding according to certain pre-established rules. This is also true of more normal forms of decoding such as the one required to understand the Morse code.

7 Stanley Fish, *Is There a Text in This Class?: The Authority of Interpretive Communities* (Cambridge, Mass.: Harvard University Press, 1980). The quotations are from pp. 327, 338, and 342, respectively. Further quotations from this work will be given parenthetically in the text.

8 Susan L. Feagin, "Incompatible Interpretations of Art," *Philosophy and Literature* 6 (1982): 133–46. My reference is to p. 139.

9 Cf. the comment in Thom, *Making Sense*, 37, that for the interpreter "the object's indeterminacy marks a failure" to be remedied, and David Novitz's observation that we interpret "in order to fill gaps in our understanding," in "Interpretation and Justification" in Margolis and Rockmore, eds., *The Philosophy of Interpretation*, 4–24 (the quotation is from p. 5).

10 The classic statement of this distinction is Robert Matthews, "Describing and Interpreting a Work of Art," *Journal of Aesthetics and Art Criticism* 36 (1977): 5–14. Barnes, *On Interpretation*, chs. 2, 3, and 8, introduces nuances and complications, but without challenging the basic idea that we do not interpret that which is transparently knowable. Cf. also the insistence in Peter Lamarque, "Objects of Interpretation," in Margolis and Rockmore, eds., *The Philosophy of Interpretation*, 96–124, that "[i]nterpretation begins only at the level where genuine alternative hypotheses about meaning present themselves" (99).

11 Since this is a gray area I cannot object violently to Staffan Carlshamre's list, in this volume, of different types of interpretive movement from what is manifest to what is hidden. However, at the beginning of the list I would prefer to say, for instance, that seeing a certain visual configuration as a letter in our alphabet is an exercise in automatic proficiency rather than an interpretation. Cf. Peter Lamarque's comment quoted in the preceding note.

12 Needless to say, this is a rough sketch (and the terms "analogism" and "differentialism" my own). For extended examples of the two positions, see, respectively, Noël Carroll, "Art, Intention, and Conversation," in Gary Iseminger, ed., *Intention and Interpretation* (Philadelphia: Temple University Press, 1992), 97–131; and John M. Ellis, *The Theory of Literary Criticism: A Logical Analysis* (Berkeley and Los Angeles: University of California Press, 1977), particularly 42–48 and 107–13, as well as Peter Lamarque and Stein Haugom Olsen, *Truth, Fiction and Literature: A Philosophical Perspective* (Oxford: Clarendon Press, 1994).

2

Five Kinds of Literary and Artistic Interpretation

Anders Pettersson

1. PRELIMINARIES

The objective of this essay is to develop and substantiate the idea that interpretations in the aesthetic disciplines are of many different types, and that that fact is of considerable importance for the theory of interpretation. First I shall, later in this section, introduce two artworks: Kafka's short story "The Judgement" and Manet's painting *A Bar at the Folies-Bergère*. Using actual critical statements about those works as examples, I shall then point to five kinds of interpretive activities that follow partly different rules (section 2). Finally, I shall argue that the concept of interpretation is comprehensive enough to cover all these activities and that one cannot, therefore, without serious consequences, ignore the multiplicity of interpretation in one's thinking about what interpretation is or should be (section 3).

It is worth emphasizing from the outset that my typology of interpretation is meant to be seen neither as exhaustive, nor as the only sensible version as far as it goes, nor as useful for all purposes. (Cf. Staffan Carlshamre's "Types of Types of Interpretation," below, where Carlshamre makes it evident that the aims of such typologies may differ widely.) My main ambition is to give a clearer perception of the multiplicity of interpretation and the consequences of this diversity, and discerning five kinds of interpretation is primarily designed to be of assistance in that context. Nonetheless, the typology is naturally meant to draw attention to some genuinely important divisions, thus elucidating the conditions of the interpretation of literature and art.

In the essay, I use the word "interpretation" as an approximate synonym for "meaning assignment." Thus I speak of the interpretation of literature and art both in connection with the ascription to a text or an artwork of a literal or representational meaning, of a symbolic import, of a certain theme, and so on. (I shall attempt to explain and justify this usage – which may appear somewhat too broad – in section 3.)

It has already been pointed out that interpretation may be divided into kinds according to several different principles. The basis of division employed here is functional, not formal: I classify interpretations starting from the purposes behind them. The purposes are said to be different, and to give rise to interpretations that are of different kinds, when the interpretations obviously do not have to meet requirements that are of the same character, i.e., when they differ with respect to their principal acceptability conditions.

These stipulations still leave room for a great number of diverse typologies of interpretation, but it should be kept in mind that I do not pretend to be constructing a typology which can claim universal validity. My pretensions are more modest: to introduce an illuminating typology which, at the same time, convincingly illustrates the multiplicity of interpretation.

The distinctions between five kinds of interpretation outlined in section 2 below are constructed on a few basic assumptions about the practice or practices surrounding the reading of literature and the viewing of art. First, I take it for granted that literary texts and works of visual art are created in order to be read/viewed and enjoyed. Second, I presuppose that reading/viewing and enjoying (or disliking) are precisely what we are involved in when we encounter and interpret such works on a non-professional basis, as ordinary readers or viewers. Third, I contend that the professional, especially academic, study of literature and art should be seen as a different practice or set of practices. True, scholars or critics must naturally base themselves on an "ordinary" reading or viewing experience. What the scholar or critic seeks, *qua* scholar or critic, is, however, not personal enjoyment of the aesthetic or artistic values that the work may afford. The objective of scholars or critics must rather be to produce either pertinent knowledge about the work or pertinent perspectives on it, and this places their interpretations in a different practical and theoretical context from those of ordinary readers or viewers, giving them a partly dissimilar character and other acceptability conditions. (Indirectly, of course, the critic's provision of knowledge or perspectives may well serve to enhance the ordinary reader's or viewer's enjoyment, and may even have this as its principal purpose, but that is another matter.) In the light of these considerations, it appears natural to me to draw the principal distinction between interpretation related to ordinary reading or viewing on the one hand and professional, especially academic, interpretation on the other.

I shall further describe the ordinary reader's or viewer's interpretation or understanding of a work as having a dual nature: as being both a construction or *reconstruction* of the public, largely convention-bound, meaning of the work and a mostly personal reaction to, or *assimilation* of, that meaning. Where the ends of academic interpretation are concerned, they are so multifarious that I shall not even attempt here to sketch an all-round picture of them. In this essay, I shall stress the difference between author-, work-, and reader-orientated interpretations: between interpretations primarily relating the work to its personal or social background (the author, the intellectual milieu, the social conditions), interpretations concentrated on "the work itself," and interpretations whose real aim is to suggest a way of reading or viewing the work. The respective orientations will be exemplified by three kinds of interpretations that I call *retrieval of representational intentions (for the sake of explanation)*, *structural analysis*, and *exposition of focal aspects*.

These terms and conceptions will be made clearer in the later discussion. Let me also add three more observations before I proceed to the Kafka and Manet examples.

I should like to point out that my discussion of types of academic interpretation has nothing to do with the differences between various schools or -isms in the aesthetic disciplines. Classical structuralist interpretation, Marxist interpretation, psychoanalytical interpretation, deconstructionist interpretation, and so on, could no doubt with some justification be seen as more or less self-contained systems of interpretation, each with its own suppositions and rules. I have not, however, adopted that perspective, mainly because I do not want to foster the impression that approaches like the ones mentioned are incommensurable in the final analysis. The ordinary reading or viewing of literature or art as it exists today can, I believe, with actual empirical justification be regarded as a distinctive cultural practice that has relatively loose boundaries but nevertheless exhibits substantial unity. I see the academic study of literature and art, in its turn, as supervening on this practice, explaining and, in a sense, enlarging it, and as facing, in doing so, a multitude of partly separate tasks, established by tradition and continuously reformulated. Seen from that perspective, different theoretical and methodological persuasions and strategies stand out as sometimes conflicting, sometimes complementary attempts to come to grips with the legitimate problems of the academic student of literature or art – not as self-sufficient techniques but as intellectual alternatives, whose merits and deficiencies are open to rational discussion.

It is also important for me to stress that there is no normative intention behind my proposals. The main contention in this essay is that there are palpable differences between the things usually called interpretations of literature and art. Those differences may certainly be described in many ways. Although I hope that the typology introduced here is clarifying, I regard it merely as one such description. (My typology puts the stress especially on the difference between the two basic practices referred to above, and also on the diversity of the tasks confronting academic scholarship and criticism, while I bypass many other interesting divergences.) Nor do I advocate any special kind of interpretation. The gist of my argument is, rather, that there are many legitimate kinds of interpretations, and that perceiving the actual multiplicity of what we call interpretation helps us to do justice to the complexity of the task of understanding literature and art.

Finally, despite my insistence on the plurality of kinds of meaning-assignment, I in no way deny that there is an underlying unity in artistic and literary interpretation, or that such interpretation can, when described in broad outline, be seen as a coherent whole. The perspective is natural and well known: The text or the work of visual art has a meaning; interpretation is the presentation of that meaning.[1] What I say below is wholly compatible with such views, but it is not the object of my essay to call attention to what is true in them or to explore what holds the concept of interpretation together. My aim, instead, is to underscore something in reality less well understood: that blanket terms like "meaning" and, especially, "interpretation" also cover a diversity that one cannot afford to overlook if one is interested in understanding and practising interpretation.

As already indicated, I shall be making frequent use of Franz Kafka's short story "The Judgement" ("Das Urteil," 1913), of Édouard Manet's painting *A Bar at the Folies-Bergère* (*Un Bar aux Folies-Bergère*, 1881–82), and of some critics' and scholars' observations about them, in order to explain my standpoints and make them more concrete.[2]

The protagonist of Kafka's story – one of the few works that the author published during his lifetime (1883–1924) – is a young businessman living with his old, weak, widowed father, whose firm he has now taken over. The story opens on a fine morning in spring:

It was a Sunday morning in the height of spring. Georg Bendemann, a young businessman, was sitting in his own room on the first floor of one of the small, lightly built houses which stretched out in a long row beside the river, hardly distinguishable from one another except in height and colour. He had just finished a letter to an old friend of his who was now living abroad, toyed with it for a while as he slowly sealed it, and then, resting his elbow on his desk, he looked out of the window at the river, the bridge and the rising ground on the far bank with its faint show of green.[3]

The young man has a fiancée and intends to marry her. In the letter he has just sealed, he informs his absent friend of this – a step he has long hesitated to take. But before posting the letter, Georg goes to his father's room and tells him that he has now written to the friend about the engagement. At that point, the realistic story undergoes a fantastic reversal. The father begins to scold and abuse his son – according to the father, Georg has betrayed both him and his deceased mother in courting his fiancée and committing other vicious acts. The confrontation escalates to the point where the infuriated old man sentences Georg to death by drowning. At the end of the story we find the obedient Georg rushing out of the house in order to drown himself in the river across the street:

Out of the front door he sprang, across the roadway, towards the water he was driven. Already he was grasping at the railings as a starving man grasps at food. He swung himself over, like the outstanding gymnast who had once been his parents' pride. Still holding on, with a weakening grip, he spied through the railings a motor-bus that would easily cover the noise of his fall, called out softly: "Dear parents, I did always love you," and let himself drop.

At that moment the traffic was passing over the bridge in a positively unending stream.[4]

"The Judgement" has been understood in very different ways. When reading the story, I myself tend to focus on how the protagonist is, in part, the helpless and irrational victim of dependences obviously developed in his childhood. To me, the story seems to emphasize both the strength and the absurdity of these ties, and I am vaguely reminded of parallels in my own life. Unlike most professional readers,

Figure 1. Édouard Manet, *Un Bar aux Folies-Bergère*, 1881–82. Oil on canvas. Courtauld Institute Galleries, London. (Bradford R. Collins, *Twelve Views of Manet's Bar*. Copyright 1996 by Princeton University Press.) Reprinted by permission of Princeton University Press

who tend to display little appreciation of the story, I find "The Judgement" powerful and strangely liberating.

"The Judgement" is an early work and is often seen as Kafka's first piece of writing in his mature style; Kafka himself always valued it highly. The entire story was written during a single night of intense labour. As is obvious from Kafka's diary and from everything else we know about his situation, "The Judgement" was decisively inspired by Kafka's recent encounter with Felice Bauer, a woman who was to play a significant role in his life and also become his fiancée for a few months. The story is even dedicated to Felice.[5]

The *Bar at the Folies-Bergère* (see figure 1) is considered to be Manet's last major work and one of his masterpieces. When he painted the *Bar* in 1881–82, Manet was around fifty – he was born in 1832 – and partly disabled by physical ailments caused by his syphilis. He was to die in 1883.

The Folies-Bergère of Manet's time has been described as "a synthesis of fashionable promenade, café-concert, and theater."[6] In Manet's painting we see a woman tending a bar, apparently a bar on the

Figure 2. Jules Chéret, *Aux Folies-Bergère*, 1875. Colour lithograph. Private collection. (Collins, *Twelve Views of Manet's Bar*. Copyright 1996 by Princeton University Press.) Reprinted by permission of Princeton University Press

right-hand side on the balcony (cf. figure 2).[7] A mirror behind her reflects the bar, the other side of the horseshoe-shaped balcony and, below, a portion of the ground floor.

At first glance the painting may seem simple and straightforward enough, but on closer inspection it becomes evident that Manet has taken the liberty of disregarding the laws of optics to a surprising extent. The opposite side of the balcony appears to be quite close to us, for example, and there seems to be no room at all between the bar and

40901

UNE MARCHANDE DE CONSOLATION AUX FOLIES-BERGÈRE. — (Son dos se reflète dans une glace; mais, sans doute par suite d'une distraction du peintre, un monsieur avec lequel elle cause et dont on voit l'image dans la glace, n'existe pas dans le tableau. — Nous croyons devoir réparer cette omission.)

Figure 3. Stop, *Édouard Manet, Une Marchande de consolation aux Folies-Bergère.* Wood engraving in *Le Journal amusant*, 27 May 1882. The French text reads: "A WOMAN SELLING CONSOLATION AT THE FOLIES-BERGÈRE. – (Her back is reflected in a mirror; but, no doubt due to some distraction of the painter, a man with whom she is conversing, and whose image is seen in the mirror, does not exist in the painting. – We think we should repair the omission.)" (Collins, *Twelve Views of Manet's Bar.* Copyright 1996 by Princeton University Press.) Reprinted by permission of Princeton University Press

the gaping precipice where the balcony ends.[8] The arrangement of the bottles to the left differs noticeably from that of their mirror images. And so forth.

Most remarkable of all: judging from the reflection, the woman appears to be serving a customer. He is not, however, seen in the picture (nor does the woman's posture in the mirror agree exactly with that in the scene).[9] That was an "oversight" which provoked amusement among Manet's contemporaries when his *Bar* was exhibited at the *Salon* of 1882 (cf. Stop's engraving, figure 3).

Manet could, of course, easily have constructed an optically realistic representation of barmaid, customer, and mirror image. But as I see it, the emotional focal point of the painting is the barmaid's face, whose melancholy air introduces a note of emptiness and nothingness. If the woman's facial expression is indeed of central importance, then it is understandable that Manet has not impeded our view of it by placing a customer in front of her as Stop does, or by making her look sideways at a merely mirrored customer as in a painted sketch of his own.[10]

Superficially, however, the Folies-Bergère is meant to appear as an attractive place full of amusements (note the trapeze artist's legs in the upper left hand corner), people, and sensuous pleasures. For that reason, we must be made to feel the presence of the audience on the opposite side of the balcony, and the woman cannot be left standing completely alone at her bar: we are to perceive that she is lonely and sad in a temple of pleasure seething with people; in fact, in the midst of a transaction with a customer.[11] These conflicting demands explain, to my mind, why Manet chose to depart from realism and settle for the compromise solution that the finished painting represents. And it would certainly have been a mistake to work out the mirror reflections meticulously. The discreet impression of unreality created by Manet's sketchy and inconsistent rendering fits the theme wonderfully well.

2. ORDINARY READING/VIEWING AND CRITICAL/SCHOLARLY ANALYSIS

After this brief look at two works by Kafka and Manet, it is time to move on to our main subject: interpretation. In that context, I would first of all like to suggest that the ordinary reader or viewer is always simultaneously engaged in two rather different activities. In responding to Manet's *Bar*, for example, you reconstruct the depicted interior – among other things, you infer or reconstruct what objects the paint patterns on the canvas are meant to represent – but you also allow the painting to affect you, reacting to the bar scene with implicit or explicit thoughts or feelings that together constitute an aesthetic experience.

Reconstruction, as it will be called here, is in my opinion best understood as an attempt to infer the artist's representational intentions (in this case, infer how the painter intended viewers to construe the representational content of the image): the viewer implicitly considers the artist's possible intentions when she mentally transforms the patterns of paint into a visualized scene. It seems to me that this is the only natural way of comprehending what the viewer actually does. Think, for example, of the words "Manet 1882" that can be read on the label of the bottle at the far left on the counter. Presumably, every competent viewer understands them as the signature and dating of the painting (and their placing as a kind of unobtrusive visual joke). But that understanding must reasonably rest on a tacit assumption about how the traits are *meant* to be taken: in principle, nothing would prevent us from seeing the words as forming part of the represented scenery, as words printed on the label and specifying the name and vintage of the wine. Surely this interpretation cannot be a deduction from the look of the painting and some sort of visual meaning conventions. Nor is it plausible to explain it as a reading created by the viewer of his own will – not if it is indeed the way every competent observer understands the trait.

The merits of intentionalism, or of the variety of it just suggested, are, however, not actually at stake here. My real contention is the less controversial one that there is, by and large, an *adequate* way of reconstructing a text or a painting, and consequently many ways of *mis*understanding such works.[12] If someone seriously believes that the bar in *A Bar at the Folies-Bergère* is represented as having a bottle of Manet 1882 for sale, she has partially misconstrued the content of the painting.

Note that I do not propose that we should regard a reader's or viewer's reconstruction as adequate when and only when he apprehends the text's or painting's representational content in the way that the author or artist meant it to be perceived. For one thing, the originator may simply have failed to make his or her intention recoverable. It is conceivable, for example, that Kafka may have wanted "The Judgement" to be enacted on a Monday morning, but have written "Sunday" by mistake and not noticed the error later. Even if that were the case (which is, of course, highly improbable), the competent reader would still be justified in construing the story as taking place on a Sunday. For an adequate reconstruction should, arguably, be based on the *most reasonable* hypothesis about the author's representational intentions, which is not necessarily the *true* hypothesis about them.[13]

It is natural, then, to characterize the ordinary reader's or viewer's interpretation as adequate or inadequate as long as one is thinking of its reconstructive aspect only. Confronted with "The Judgement" or the *Bar*, we do not, though, confine ourselves to the reconstruction of their representational content. We also apply what we read or see to our present situation, deriving insights, or aesthetic satisfaction, or emotional gratification in the process. The enjoyment that a work affords inevitably varies from person to person, and questions of adequacy are normally regarded as marginal in this connection. Different people simply get partially different things out of reading "The Judgement" or viewing the *Bar*. In a sense, the responses of experienced readers and viewers will no doubt tend to be more competent than those of other people – more circumspect and nuanced. But to speak of correctness seems somewhat out of place. It is perhaps more apposite to say that reactions to art can be more or less perceptive and mature, just like reactions to everyday situations, to moral dilemmas, and so on.[14]

Thus, reading/viewing and understanding an artwork comprises both reconstruction and what I shall call *assimilation*. My reason for seeing reconstruction and assimilation as different *kinds* of interpretation is, simply, that their acceptability conditions cannot easily be the same. Reconstruction is a question of attempting to grasp the originator's representational intentions and can be assessed as being adequate or inadequate. Assimilation is largely a personal matter where correctness does not come into the picture (but rather such things as receptivity, imaginativeness, or maturity).[15] A reconstruction is, in reason, valid if it is plausible taken as a mirroring of the content of the originator's representational intentions. A good assimilation, on the other hand, is mainly required to forge a productive connection between the reconstructed content and the reader's or viewer's needs and interests.

As I have already emphasized, literary texts are written to be read and enjoyed and paintings are created to be viewed and responded to. Ordinary reading or viewing is an integral part of this basic literary or artistic language game.

Scholarly and critical interpretation is something different, a secondary activity with aims and motivations of its own. Unlike the ordinary reader's or viewer's reconstructions and assimilations, it is not immediately aimed at the enjoyment of the pleasures that the artwork may afford. Its point is, rather, to enhance our understanding of the work in various ways.

Scholarship and criticism with reference to literature and art are typically concerned with clarifying their history, or with explicating individual works or *œuvres*, or with theorizing about the art form itself. Interpretation, i.e., the ascription of meaning to a work, may enter into all those tasks. Interpretation may thus have varying functions and, of course, also rest on different theoretical and methodological convictions. The just assessment of a critical or scholarly interpretive remark therefore presupposes a clear understanding of its context, purpose, and pretensions. Often, much of that relevant background is left unspecified by the interpreter, which poses serious obstacles for the analyst.[16]

Owing mainly to these complications, I will not attempt to establish an overall classification of kinds of interpretation in critical/scholarly analysis. As I said earlier, I shall content myself with indicating, and commenting on, the three broad and significantly differing types which I call *retrieval of representational intentions (for the sake of explanation)*, *structural analysis*, and *exposition of focal aspects*. Interpretations of "The Judgement" will be used for exemplification.

In describing various sorts of historical developments, the historian of literature or art often naturally resorts to explanations of a causal or teleological (intention-oriented) kind. The retrieval and description of the author's or artist's representational intentions can function as one variety of such explanation, one way of making clear why the work has acquired the properties it possesses. Thus Hartmut Binder writes in "The Background" (1977), a description of the biographical realities behind Kafka's "The Judgement":

> … Kafka's own interpretation of the course of the narrative makes clear that "The Judgment" has as its subject a father-son relationship, and this is supported by two additional factors. Firstly, Kafka intended to publish the story together with "The Stoker" and "Metamorphosis" in a collection entitled *Sons*. On the 11th of April, 1913, he wrote to his publisher, Kurt Wolff, that there existed "an obvious, and, more important, a secret bond" between those three texts, and he definitely wanted to present them together. An analogy is especially apparent between "The Judgement" and "Metamorphosis," where one finds not only affinity of motif but also similarity of structure. …
>
> Further proof for the idea that Kafka in "The Judgment" thematized the conflict of the generations can be deduced from the thoughts in Kafka's mind as he was writing: "thoughts about Freud, of course; in one passage, of

Arnold Beer [a novel by Max Brod]; in another, of Wassermann; in another, *smash*, of Werfel's giantess; of course, also of my 'The Urban World'." ...

The formulation shows that Kafka quite automatically connects the story as a whole with the teachings of Freud, familiar to him in various forms; the doctrine is centered totally on the Oedipus complex, that is, on the son's hatred, fear, respect, rebellion, and the will to power.[17]

When Binder declares that the story's subject or theme is "a father-son relationship," he is making an interpretive remark. It is natural to understand him as speaking of the complex of representations linguistically communicated to us and pointing to its central aspect. Binder is, however, exclusively concerned with Kafka's view of the story. What matters to him is to make clear how Kafka saw "The Judgement." In saying that the story's subject or theme is "a father-son relationship," Binder is effectively asserting that the aspect in question was the one that was central to Kafka.

It is possible to regard Binder as an out-and-out intentionalist convinced that the theme of a literary work is the aspect that its author intends to foreground. If understood in that spirit, he is retrieving Kafka's representational intentions in order to expose the story's focal aspects. However, Binder can also be interpreted – more charitably, perhaps – simply as being occupied, in the article from which I quote, with explanation, more precisely with expounding why Kafka wrote the story the way he did. I am inclined to understand Binder mainly in the latter fashion (it is a thorny question exactly how his remarks are to be interpreted; cf. note 16 above), particularly because of the title and context of his article. Binder's words about the story's subject or theme are then to be taken primarily as an elliptical statement about what the story meant to Kafka and as presupposing no controversial ideas about meaning and interpretation. (Thus conceived, Binder's formulations do not necessarily conflict with my own reading of the story, focused on the somewhat wider issue of how the protagonist is motivated, mostly against his wishes, by dependences developed in his childhood.)

Binder's interpretive remark appears to me to be intended as an ordinary statement, capable of being true or false in the everyday sense,[18] and I see no reason why the remark should not be construed in that manner. Kafka must surely have understood his story one way or another (even if his ideas about it may have been vague and variable), so it would be a meaningful question to ask to what extent Binder's description of Kafka's view of "The Judgement" was correct.

Retrievals of representational intentions – whether they are made for explanatory or expository purposes – are thus, in principle, assessable as true or false, and in this they differ from both reconstructions and assimilations. Let us now consider another type of interpretive remark about "The Judgement": structural analysis. A piece of structural analysis takes the verbal sign-sequence or the complex of communicated representations as its starting-point. Unlike reconstruction, however, structural analysis does not merely seek to establish the text and the content but also to describe their characteristics. Structural analysis may be undertaken for various purposes. The ambition behind it, for example, may be to disclose structural patterns characteristic of a work, an author, a genre, or a period, or to lay the foundation for a literary comparison, or to explain a work's effectiveness by revealing hidden qualities that possibly influence our response.

In a book-length study of aspects of Kafka's narrative technique (1971), Klaus Ramm discusses the iterative dimension of a dialogue figuring in Kafka's story. He does this in order to support his claim that the temporal structure of Kafka's fictional worlds is fundamentally non-linear and should be characterized as that of an everlasting moment.[19]

The dialogue in question concerns Georg Bendemann's frail and sensitive relationship with the friend living abroad, the one to whom he has been writing on the fateful Sunday morning. Georg has long hesitated to tell his friend about his forthcoming wedding.

> He [Georg] often talked to his fiancée of this friend of his, and of the special relationship which he had with him owing to their correspondence. "So he won't be coming to our wedding," said she, "and yet I have a right to get to know all your friends." "I don't want to disturb him," Georg replied, "don't misunderstand me, he probably would come, at least I think so, but he would feel awkward and at a disadvantage, perhaps even envious of me, at all events he would be dissatisfied, and with no prospect of ever ridding himself of his dissatisfaction he'd have to go back again alone. Alone – do you realize what that means?" "Yes, but may he not hear about our wedding in some other way?" "I can't prevent that, certainly, but it's unlikely if you consider his circumstances." "If you've got friends like that, Georg, you should never have

got engaged." "Well, we're both of us to blame there; but I wouldn't have it any other way now." And when, breathing faster under his kisses, she still objected: "All the same, it does upset me," he thought it really couldn't do any harm to tell his friend the whole story. "That's how I'm made and he must just take me as I am," he said to himself, "I can't fashion myself into a different kind of person who might perhaps make him a more suitable friend."[20]

Kafka first tells us that the subject of Georg's friend "often" came up between Georg and his fiancée, and then he lets us listen to a conversation between Georg and Frieda (as she is called). Binder has commented (in a different contribution from the one cited earlier) that the conversation reads like the rendition of a single, isolated event but is given the task of showing the typical structure of all the dialogues in question. Ramm has two objections to that rather unremarkable observation. First, he does not find it evident that the conversation has the task of showing the typical structure of all those dialogues. Second, he considers that it is impossible to say whether only one specific conversation is being represented in the passage. In particular, he points out that the sentence which begins, in the English translation, "And when, breathing faster under his kisses," has been given an iterative formulation (Kafka employs *wenn*, not *als*, as the temporal conjunction).[21]

According to Ramm, then, but not to Binder, just on how many occasions Georg and Frieda have said these words is an open question. Obviously, Binder and Ramm differ slightly in their preferred reconstructions, more precisely in their views of what is the case in the story world. (I myself side with Binder.)[22] But Ramm also uses his reconstruction to support a piece of structural analysis. To Ramm, the dialogue exemplifies a feature typical of Kafka, a "structure, in which a seemingly unique occurrence cannot be distinguished from its own iteration."[23]

Again, it appears incontestable to me that we are dealing with an interpretive remark. Ramm's last observation does not concern semantic meaning, the text's denotational core, but connotations concerning the tone, perspective, or atmosphere in "The Judgement." Ramm can thus be said to be discussing form rather than content. Nevertheless, he attempts to point to one of the meaning-creating features in Kafka's story, one of the traits supposedly responsible for our picture of the story's world, and to indicate its effects, at least approximately.

As I understand it, a structural analysis such as Ramm's makes three kinds of claims which must all be acceptable if the analysis is to be valid. First, underlying the analysis there is an ordinary reconstruction whose adequacy is presupposed. Second, it is contended that the reconstructed text or content can justly be described in a certain way (here: that a scene in the story is a seemingly unique occurrence which cannot, however, be distinguished from its own iteration). Third, the indicated feature is supposed to be instrumental, to some degree at least, in eliciting a relevant literary experience. The complex acceptability condition just outlined sets structural analysis clearly apart from reconstruction, assimilation, and retrieval of representational intentions.

When talking about interpretation of a literary or artistic composition, we are, however, undoubtedly most often thinking of the exposition of focal aspects, of general explication of what is assumed to be the overall meaning of the work. One such brief interpretation of "The Judgement" is found in *Kafka* (1967), a popular presentation of Kafka's works by Charles Osborne. Osborne retells the story and then goes on to write:

George is destroyed, not by his father's mad judgement, but by his friend in St Petersburg or, to be more exact, by the inadequacy of his relationship with his friend in St Petersburg. Or, in other words, by the inadequacy of the relationship between his conscious self and his unconscious. George's inner condition is beyond the possibility of healing or recovery. His self-confident success is meaningless. His refusal to face himself in the mirror of reality, symbolised by his keeping his friend at a great distance in a foreign country, destroys him. His father, whom we see only through George's extremely subjective vision, destroys him only in that he completely understands him. And George destroys himself, too, when, too late, self-knowledge is forced upon him. The struggle, whether between father and son or between Ego and Id is, as always with Kafka, the struggle between the devitalised, aimless existence, devoid of conscience or of free-will, and the harder, almost impossible road where each step forward is painful, whose end may be insanity, nothingness or creation, but whose way is at any rate the way of responsibility and awareness. At the moment of crisis, George fails. His flinging himself into the river was the final act of irresponsibility, though perhaps one should blame God, the father. Certainly if one inclines to see the father as God and the dead mother as the diminished power of the church or synagogue, the man is alone, self-confidently alone in his decisions until pulled up short by the necessarily irrational behaviour of God. Thus God destroys man.[24]

In this passage, Osborne describes or redescribes the story. He highlights the features that he finds aesthetically or artistically essential, while also explaining what they stand for and how they are related. Precisely those features are the defining properties of what I call an exposition of focal aspects. In other respects, the character of such expositions is variable. Expositions of focal aspects may, for example, be much more succinct or much more extensive, or concentrate on formal aspects rather than on thematic ones. (I would have spoken of "thematic exposition" instead of "exposition of focal aspects," had it not been the case that it is precisely the formal, non-thematic aspects that are crucial in some kinds of literature and art; for example, in non-figurative painting.)

The reconstructed world of a text or painting may be approached and evaluated in very different ways. Within certain limits – which I shall not attempt to demarcate here – all such diverging readings appear defensible to me (even when I personally do not find them useful or interesting). Texts and paintings are created to be encountered and experienced, and at least where works from the last 150 years or so are concerned, the possibility of their being apprehended in rather different ways could with some justification be said to be implicitly foreseen and accepted by their originators.

Obviously, Osborne's interpretive remarks do not essentially aspire to describe Kafka's own understanding of the story. In this they differ from Binder's and resemble Ramm's. But since Osborne is indicating a possible assimilation of "The Judgment" rather than reconstructing the story, his remarks are much more definitely stamped as constructions than are those of Ramm. It is not unnatural to see remarks like Ramm's as true or false (even if that would, in the final analysis, not be quite to the point). It seems more apposite to speak of expositions of focal aspects such as Osborne's as illuminating or indifferent, or as natural or strained.

This is not surprising, since exposition of focal aspects must be closely related to assimilation: Osborne's remarks indicate a way of seeing the story that may well underlie some actual reader responses (his own, for example). But an exposition of focal aspects nevertheless has a different purpose, and consequently has to meet other requirements. Assimilations must above all be meaningful to those who make them. To expose focal aspects is not to experience the work, nor is it to merely report one's own personal thoughts or feelings in the face of it. True, the pretensions associated with such expositions may in fact differ considerably. To borrow a formulation from Robert Stecker, these interpretations may aim at "understanding a work as the product, for the most part, of design by its historical creator," or at "enhancing the aesthetic value of a work, or at making the work more relevant to the interpreter's contemporaries, or at just offering an interesting way of reading the work."[25] Unlike assimilations, though, they all aspire to some kind of *general* interest or significance; they claim to have something to offer the literary or artistic community as a whole. Expositions of focal aspects have a public role, while assimilations are basically of a private nature.

3. INTERPRETATION IN THE "PROPER" SENSE

In the last section I described some interpretive activities that, as I see it, may be legitimately characterized as five different kinds of interpretation: reconstruction, assimilation, retrieval of representational intentions (for the sake of explanation), structural analysis, and exposition of focal aspects. When we speak of interpretation in connection with literature and the arts, however, we tend to think mainly of what I called exposition of focal aspects. Many would no doubt wish to argue that only such expositions – and not reconstructions, assimilations, explanations, or structural analyses – are interpretations in the proper sense.

In this section, I attempt to answer objections of that kind. First I provide some additional examples of expositions of focal aspects (this time analyses of Manet's *Bar*) in order to support my assertion that such interpretations may be of several different types. Then I attempt to refute the identification of interpretation with the exposition of focal aspects by demonstrating that "interpretation," as the word is ordinarily used, does in fact cover considerably more than just that. In the course of the discussion, I also point to the consequences of overlooking the differences between interpretations by commenting on a couple of general statements about interpretation where what is true of focal-aspects exposition is in practice supposed to hold for all interpretation.

In his book from 1985 about Manet and his followers, T.J. Clark gives a description of the *Bar* that emphasizes its incongruities and uncertainties, and then proceeds to consider Manet's "possible intentions."[26] Clark's argument is largely implicit, but I believe that we are justified in construing it along the following lines: There is a certain opaqueness about modern bourgeois society; a person's character and class are now far less readily visually discernible than in earlier times (255). Fascinated by that fact, and seeking a hold on their contemporary realities ("a point of insertion into modern life," 258), the artistic avant-garde of Manet's day often chose the petite bourgeoisie, with its socially ambiguous situation and appearance, as a subject (ibid.). The *Bar* is an example of this. It is concerned with "social forms" (252) and focuses on the ambiguity around the barmaid.

> It is a picture of a woman in a café-concert, selling drinks and oranges, and most probably for sale herself – or believed to be so by some of her customers. ... The face she wears is the face of the popular, as previously defined, but also of a fierce, imperfect resistance to any such ascription. It is a face whose character derives from not being bourgeois, and having that fact almost be hidden. For if one could not be bourgeois – if that status was always pushed just a little further out of reach – then at least one could prevent oneself from being anything else: fashion and reserve would keep one's face from *any* identity, from identity in general. The look which results is a special one: public, outward, "blasé" in Simmel's sense, impassive, not bored, not tired, not disdainful, not quite focused on anything. Expression is its enemy, the mistake it concentrates on avoiding at all costs; for to express oneself would be to have one's class be legible.
>
> *Un Bar* is surely concerned to picture that kind of effacement, but also the actual social circumstances in which it took place and which made it obligatory. (253–4)

Clark's much-discussed interpretation has been emphatically rejected by, among others, Bradford R. Collins. In an article in the collection of essays about the *Bar* that he edited in 1996, Collins argues that Clark and those who share his views "suggest that Manet's painting is ultimately a kind of sociological mirror."[27] However, modern psychology makes it obvious, says Collins, that the artist does not simply record realities but works "to achieve some personal satisfaction, address some need or needs" (124). Collins then sets out "to demonstrate that the work mirrors, instead, Manet's deepest and long-standing convictions about the male condition" (133).[28] According to Collins, the *Bar* enters into a dialogue with what he calls "the Venetian tradition" (see esp. 127–9), an art tradition defined by its portayal of women as welcoming the male gaze and responding positively to it. Manet, on the contrary, underlines the "barmaid's inaccessibility" (120) – possibly because of his "pessimistic convictions on relations between the sexes" (129). So the "precise theme" of the picture, Collins maintains, is "an unexplained disappointment of carefully cultivated male expectations" (121). "Our masculine gaze, which at first seems to penetrate the depths of the establishment's interior space (the sexual connotation is real, I think), is actually rebuffed by the mirror and thrown back on itself" (120).

Perhaps a theme like the one suggested by Collins would seem likely to depress rather than gratify Manet and other viewers (other male heterosexual viewers, at least). But, as Collins observes, "a Freudian therapist might argue that Manet's refusal to participate in the *méconnaissance* perpetuated by the Venetian tradition was healthy; the *Bar* and works like it would have strengthened his ego (as conceptualized by Freud) to bear the burden of its solitude and insufficiency" (132–3).[29]

The tacit theoretical suppositions behind Clark's and Collins's interpretations can be reconstructed in more than one way. It is, however, not unnatural to see the two interpretations as conflicting attempts to solve the same task.

Collins is convinced that the question what the work "ultimately" mirrors must be answered along psychological or psychoanalytical lines. In this, his methodological assumptions obviously differ from Clark's. But Collins's basic aim appears to be to describe the actual function of the painting – for Manet, but perhaps also for his viewers – and the same, I believe, could be said about Clark. Clark supposes, for example, that the "inconsistencies" that he perceives in the painting "must have been felt to be somehow appropriate to the social forms the painter had chosen to show."[30] In such passages he seems to be speaking, just like Collins, of the actual psychological motivation underlying Manet's work on the painting. And he appears to be saying (again like Collins) something that could in principle be characterized as true or false. (Though neither his nor Collins's statements are certainly formulated in precise and testable terms.)

A consideration of Clark's and Collins's analyses does not, then, discourage us from seeing the exposition of focal aspects as a unitary activity. But there are other such interpretations of the *Bar* that follow radically different rules. James D. Herbert has published an article where he contends, among other things, that there is no absolute, privileged position from which to view the *Bar*. In that connection, he suggests that we can imagine the picture as representing a mirror in which we see a barmaid looking at herself. "Suddenly the starkly frontal image of the barmaid takes on an entirely new meaning. Her unflinching yet diffused gaze becomes, convincingly, the look of someone examining her reflection – the reflection not just of her eyes but of her whole corporeal presence – in a mirror."[31] And he defends this "feminist reading" of the picture as "no more 'an ideological mirage'" than "the demand that we constrain ourselves to Manet's reality."[32]

If we try to view the painting in the way Herbert suggests, it appears difficult to make sense of what we see behind the woman's back (are we to imagine, for example, that there is a *painting* rather than a *mirror* hanging on the wall?), and, for that matter, also of the woman's posture, the direction of her gaze, the locality, and the situation as a whole.[33] All those problems are, however, of subordinate importance in the present context. What interests me here is simply the circumstance that Herbert's exposition of focal aspects cannot very well be taken in the same spirit as Clark's or Collins's. For as Herbert himself makes clear, his aim is not to recover Manet's intentions or his painterly or psychological motives. It is evident, instead, that he simply wishes to describe one worthwhile way of viewing the *Bar*, and thus to introduce a reading validated primarily by its own intrinsic interest. The interpretation of literature and art could not, then, be said to be a unitary activity even if we were to define "interpretation" narrowly as the exposition of the focal aspects of a literary or artistic work.

No doubt, many would disagree with this conclusion. One example of another outlook can already be found in Collins's 1996 collection of articles. There Richard Shiff reflects, in an introductory essay, on the traditions of Manet scholarship and on the approaches encountered in the anthology. The following, final passage in Shiff's essay gives a good idea of his basic standpoint on the nature of art-historical writing (including ascriptions of meaning).

On the evidence of this collection and other recent publications, it appears that many art historians are shifting from an archival or biographical method (reconstructing Manet's experience) to a more emphatically subjectivized, autobiographical method (reflecting on what the experience of Manet and his

> work means to the author). I say "more" subjectivized because the selection of an archive or set of documents, even by the most empirically oriented scholar, must already reflect a certain interest or bias.
>
> Art historians' increasingly explicit recognition of their contextual limitations – the author's own situation in discourse and inability to assume a universalizing stance – might be linked to a postmodernist carnival of language and denial of authorial control. If our art history has indeed become "new," is it not likely to parallel a chronologically "late" postmodernism? Postmodernists stress the capacity of representations to associate freely with other representations, generating new meanings at each and every instant in a limitless play of both metaphor (association by resemblance or form) and metonymy (association by position or function). In a postmodern world, the author's position must keep changing as it negotiates a field of signs. ... The writing we call "history" therefore becomes artistic, like Manet's *Bar* – a matter of historically contingent, self-reflective expression. Has it not always been?[34]

Shiff contrasts the "biographical method" with the "autobiographical" one, apparently regarding them as two ways of doing the same thing (producing art history). Understood in that manner, not only Clark's and Collins's analyses but also Herbert's would have to be seen as straightforwardly competing interpretations. (Clark and Collins would perhaps be called "biographical" and Herbert be commended as more adept in negotiating a field of signs.) My contention is, of course, on the contrary, that "reconstructing Manet's experience" and "reflecting on what the experience of Manet and his work means to the author" are two quite different tasks, the former associated with the retrieval of representational intentions and such and the latter with assimilation. As I see the matter, both pursuits are of considerable interest, though their *raisons d'être*, and the contexts where they naturally belong, are very different. Consequently, Shiff's implicit suggestion that we should keep to the latter and discard the former – a proposal partly motivated, no doubt, by a belief in the unity of what we call interpretation – appears to me to be misguided.[35] (Nor do I share Shiff's belief in a constant flux of meaning, or in the capacity of representations to generate meanings on their own, and so on, but space does not permit me to enlarge on such points of dissension here.)

There is in fact a deep-rooted tendency among critics, scholars, and aestheticians to think that the word "interpretation" denotes a single, more or less definite and circumscribed activity. But "interpretation" is in reality, in common usage, a word with a fairly wide spectrum of meanings.

True, the exposition of focal aspects appears to come to the forefront where the interpretation of literature and the arts is concerned. The *Random House Unabridged Dictionary*, for example, defines "interpretation," in the sense most interesting to us, as "an explanation of the meaning of another's artistic or creative work; an elucidation: *an interpretation of a poem.*"[36] If interpretation were the *explanation* or *elucidation* of *the* meaning associated with a work, then neither reconstructions, nor assimilations, nor structural analyses could justly be called interpretations, and the status of retrievals of representational intentions (for the sake of explanation) would appear debatable at the very least.

A closer look at the word's standard meaning will, however, reveal a more complex picture. In the *Oxford English Dictionary*, thus, the words "interpret" and "interpretation" obviously also cover at least the identification of word and sentence meaning and the silent understanding during reading or listening.[37] And it is easy to find actual concrete examples, both within and outside criticism, of "interpretation" used to include reconstruction, and perhaps also assimilation, in my sense.[38] To use "interpretation" only as a designation of the exposition of focal aspects is consequently to narrow down the meaning of the word through implicit stipulation.

It has not been shown that all the five kinds of interpretation that I singled out are normally called interpretation; the inclusion of structural analysis at least could be questioned. More examples, and more discussion, of normal usage would no doubt clarify the issue, but I have not found it necessary to enter really deeply into the matter here. What was most important to me was to demonstrate the multiplicity of what we call interpretation, even though I could only give a very rough idea about it in this context, and to point to a number of significant, and significantly different, activities associated with the ascription of meaning to texts or paintings.

Neglecting the actual diversity of meaning ascription in connection with literature and art is liable to result in serious misjudgments in interpretation and interpretation theory. The identification of interpretation with focal-aspects exposition will, for example, naturally lead one to suppose that the acceptability conditions of such exposition constitute *the* requirements that *all* ascription of meaning to works of literature and art have to meet, and many critics and theorists do in fact seem to subscribe to that belief.

Not infrequently, they even appear to think of focal-aspect expositions as being all of a kind – most often, as being irreducibly subjective in nature. Shiff's remarks, discussed above, are a good example of that tendency. And Matthew Kieran writes, criticizing Stecker: "The indeterminacies of art are open to disambiguation on the part of the spectator in multifarious ways. The point of interpretation is to provide an imaginatively rich experience which affords pleasure, interest and insight to the socially situated individual."[39] Kieran seems confident that he can tell us what *the* point of interpretation is. The kind or kinds of interpretation he has in mind are presumably assimilation and/or the varieties of focal-aspects exposition aimed – in Stecker's words – at "enhancing the aesthetic value of a work, or at making the work more relevant to the interpreter's contemporaries, or at just offering an interesting way of reading the work."

Aleida Assmann, to mention a third and last example, has described the history of interpretation as leading up to a deconstructive position that resists the "communication compulsion" and the urge to understand,[40] to "a desemanticizing reading, where meanings are no longer collected but decomposed into their constituent parts" (549). Assmann speaks as if she believed that this ambition really "guides individual reading processes" in our time, i.e., "in the postmodern era" (535). Apparently, Assmann is also convinced that ordinary readers do exactly what the critic does, though the critic does it better. ("Just like theologians or jurists, literary scholars are professional readers who claim to read better than other literate people according to the rules of a certain practice," 536.)

In my opinion, Shiff, Kieran, Assmann, and many others fail to take the diversified character of literary and artistic interpretation into account. It would be unwise to repudiate subjective interpretation in general, or to condemn without reservation artificial or even "desemanticizing" readings of literature and art. But such meaning assignments should certainly not be thought to represent interpretation *tout court* – nor should any other kind.

To sum up the discussion in this section: the exposition of focal aspects is, in itself, of more than one type. Focal-aspects expositions of various sorts may be what we primarily think and speak of as literary and artistic interpretation. But we have also seen that other kinds of what is commonly called interpretation follow different principles; obviously there is no *unitary* analysis of interpretation to be had. It must logically be important for both practising critics and pure theorists to be able to keep different kinds of interpretation apart and to cultivate an awareness of their respective peculiarities.

NOTES

1 This is not the only possible description of what is common to interpretation – an interestingly different conception of the matter is presented in Paul Thom, *Making Sense: A Theory of Interpretation* (Lanham: Rowman and Littlefield, 2000), esp. 19–20.

2 It is important to remember that the two works, and the critical observations about them, are simply introduced as examples. It is not my ambition to enhance the critical or scholarly understanding of the Kafka story or the Manet painting. Nor should the interpretations cited necessarily be understood as representing the most important observations in the discussion about the works.

3 Franz Kafka, "The Judgement: A Story" [1913], in Franz Kafka, *The Transformation and Other Stories: Works Published During Kafka's Lifetime*, trans. and ed. Malcolm Pasley (Harmondsworth: Penguin Books, 1992), 37.

4 Ibid., 47.

5 The dedication ("Für F."; i.e., "For F.") is missing in Pasley's translation, but see, e.g., Franz Kafka, *Erzählungen*, ed. Max Brod (Frankfurt am Main: Fischer Taschenbuch Verlag, 1983), [42].

6 Albert Boime, "Manet's *A Bar at the Folies-Bergère* as an Allegory of Nostalgia," in Bradford R. Collins, ed., *Twelve Views of Manet's Bar* (Princeton: Princeton University Press, 1996), 49.

7 See Jack Flam's evaluation of the discussion about the setting in his "Looking into the Abyss: The Poetics of Manet's *A Bar at the Folies-Bergère*," in Collins, ed., *Twelve Views*, 187.

8 Cf. ibid., 165–6. As Flam aptly puts it: "in order to see the woman and bar as we do we would have to be hovering in thin air" (166).

9 We know that Manet experimented with various spatial relationships between barmaid and customer and successively departed more and more from the idea of a visually realistic mirror image. The stages involved are briefly described by Bradford R. Collins in "The Dialectics of Desire, the Narcissism of Authorship: A Male Interpretation of the Psychological Origins of Manet's *Bar*," in Collins, ed., *Twelve Views*, 117–19.

10 The sketch is reproduced, in black and white, in, e.g., Collins, ed., *Twelve Views*, [321], as fig. 1.

11 "Like the artist, she stands at the edge of an abyss, contemplating the transience of all pleasures and all things," as Jack Flam has formulated it in his study of the *Bar* (Flam, "Looking into the Abyss," 184). A related observation of Flam's concerns the *vanitas* symbolism in the picture: "The *Bar* not only contains certain traditional aspects of *vanitas* imagery, such as the mirror, the young woman, the flowers, and the fruit, but the very nature of the place that is represented – the music hall with its atmosphere of manufactured gaiety – reinforces the subject of the vanity of worldliness, of material possessions, and of sensuality"(173).

12 Also a classical conventionalist, for example – a person holding that the meaning of a work is determined exclusively by the properties of the work itself and the public semantic conventions in force – is liable to think of the viewer's reconstruction as an application of tacit but generally accepted principles. The conventionalist would certainly give a different explanation of how the viewer arrives at his conclusion about the text on the label, but would still think that there are adequate and inadequate ways of construing the detail.

13 The standpoint advocated here could be seen as a variety of so-called "hypothetical intentionalism." That position was introduced by William E. Tolhurst in his article "On What a Text Is and How It Means," *British Journal of Aesthetics* 19 (1979). It has since been developed and defended by, first and foremost, Jerrold Levinson; see especially Levinson's "Intention and Interpretation in Literature" in his book *The Pleasures of Aesthetics: Philosophical Essays* (Ithaca and London: Cornell University Press, 1996). There are at least two differences worth mentioning, though, between my position and those of Tolhurst and Levinson. First, I am a hypothetical intentionalist of sorts regarding only the kind of interpretation that I call "reconstruction." Moreover, I understand the reader and viewer as attempting to reconstruct the originator's actual representational intention as truly as possible on the basis of the accessible public evidence, not as attempting to build up the most plausible picture of the originator's representational intention given that evidence. (I lack the space, here, to give a proper explanation and justification of my position, so these remarks should only be taken as a rough indication of similarities and differences betwen my views and hypothetical intentionalism in the established sense.)

14 I am well aware that this is a controversial point: many aestheticians do in fact believe that there is not only a correct uptake of a work but also a

correct way of experiencing it. For two recent examples, see Derek Matravers, *Art and Emotion* (Oxford: Clarendon Press, 1998), 209 and 224, and Noël Carroll, "Moderate Moralism versus Moderate Autonomism," *British Journal of Aesthetics* 38 (1998): 420.

15 The distinction between reconstruction and assimilation is related to – but should not be equated with – such dichotomies as those between description and interpretation (Monroe C. Beardsley, *Aesthetics: Problems in the Philosophy of Criticism* [New York: Harcourt, Brace and World, 1958], 9–10 and 65) or meaning-pursuing interpretation and significance-pursuing criticism (E.D. Hirsch, Jr, *Validity in Interpretation* [New Haven: Yale University Press, 1967], 8–9).

16 Cf. Robert Stecker's remarks: "While in principle one can distinguish different interpretive *claims* people can make with their different truth conditions, and can further distinguish interpretive claims from other interpretive doings, it can easily be imagined that, in practice, people will not always be explicit, or clear in their own minds, about the claims they are making, nor will they always avoid making a mixed bag of claims. Thus, there will be plenty of room for interpreting interpretations." Robert Stecker, *Artworks: Definition Meaning Value* (University Park: Pennsylvania State University Press, 1997), 244.

17 Hartmut Binder, "The Background," in Angel Flores, ed., *The Problem of "The Judgment": Eleven Approaches to Kafka's Story* (New York: Gordian Press, 1977), 15–17. The text that Binder cites in the latter part of the quotation is Kafka's diary.

18 Note that I am speaking, here, about truth in the everyday sense – the sense in which you can, for example, make obviously true or false statements about how many people there are in a room.

19 Klaus Ramm, *Reduktion als Erzählprinzip bei Kafka* (Frankfurt am Main: Athenäum Verlag, 1971), 47–58.

20 Kafka, "The Judgement," 39–40.

21 Ramm, *Reduktion als Erzählprinzip*, 57–8.

22 The Kafka passage gives us good reasons to believe that the reported verbal exchange has in (fictional) fact occurred at least once. And we know that people would never, in an ordinary context, repeat such specific words and actions in exact detail, so we should not surmise that this has happened in the story world.

Literary compositions often set aside superficial logic in order to optimize their artistic efficacy. Think, for example, of the phenomenon called free indirect discourse, where two different temporal and spatial perspectives, that of the narrator and that of a fictional person, are adopted simultaneously in order to attain a satisfactory compromise between distance and closeness. In the quoted passage Kafka, with similar seeming inconsistency, describes something that has taken place several times but makes his text more vivid by depicting in detail what must obviously be taken as an individual, representative instance. (Ramm may, of course, nevertheless have a point when he maintains that the ensuing temporal ambiguity is characteristic of Kafka's style.)

23 Ramm, *Reduktion als Erzählprinzip*, 58; my translation.

24 Charles Osborne, *Kafka* (Edinburgh and London: Oliver and Boyd, 1967), 36–7.

Osborne's view could perhaps be said to lack nuances and to make the story stand out as too straightforwardly symbolic. But in its main outlines his interpretation tallies with many much more ambitious analyses. The *father = God, Georg = Jesus* analogy is in fact hinted at *en passant* in "The Judgement" itself. ("Jesus!" cries the charwoman on meeting Georg when he comes rushing down the stairs on his way to his suicide; Kafka, "The Judgement," 47.) And it is quite common to think that Georg's punishment is well deserved. See, e.g., the articles by Ellis, White, and Rolleston in Flores, ed., *The Problem of "The Judgment,"* esp. 92–3, 110–12, and 144. I myself basically share the importantly different perspective adopted by J.P. Stern in his contribution to Flores's anthology, "Guilt and the Feeling of Guilt" (see esp. 120–1, 125–6, and 130–1).

25 Robert Stecker, "Art Interpretation," *Journal of Aesthetics and Art Criticism* 52 (1994): 194. Stecker is speaking of interpretation in general, but I take him as referring, in reality, to the kind of interpretation called here exposition of focal aspects.

26 T.J. Clark, *The Painting of Modern Life: Paris in the Art of Manet and His Followers* (New York: Alfred A. Knopf, 1985), 252. In the rest of the paragraph, page references to Clark's book are given in parentheses in the text.

27 Collins, "The Dialectics of Desire," 123. Page references in the next few paragraphs refer to Collins's text.

28 Clark could easily argue that Manet did indeed address a need and seek personal satisfaction; for example, that Manet consciously or unconsciously attempted to achieve a satisfactory understanding of the social realities surrounding him. For that reason, Collins's argument against Clark appears oversimplified to me (as does his talk of mirroring).

29 As is evident from what was said in section 1 above, I myself do not share either Clark's or Collins's view of what constitutes the artistically or aesthetically most significant aspects of the painting. The respective merits of different ways of experiencing the *Bar* are, however, not really at issue here.

30 Clark, *The Painting of Modern Life*, 252.

31 James D. Herbert, "Privilege and the Illusion of the Real," in Collins, ed., *Twelve Views*, 225.

32 Ibid., 229.

33 In *Picture for Women* (1979), an intriguing photograph by Jeff Wall that alludes to Manet's *Bar*, we find ourselves (in the guise of a camera) looking into a mirror together with the woman at the counter. A consideration of Wall's photo makes it clear how selectively Herbert has worked out the interpretive option that he introduces.

Wall's photograph is reproduced and discussed in Thierry de Duve's "Survey: The Mainstream and the Crooked Path," in Thierry de Duve, Arielle Pelenc, and Boris Groys, *Jeff Wall* (London: Phaidon, 1996), 30–4.

34 Richard Shiff, "Introduction: Ascribing to Manet, Declaring the Author," in Collins, ed., *Twelve Views*, 19.

35 Shiff seems to think that biographical and autobiographical art history are not really cognitively compatible, so that we cannot, without inconsistency, sometimes engage in the one, sometimes in the other kind of writing. As for myself, however, I cannot detect any non-trivial incompatibility between them. (Assimilation, explanation, etc. may naturally compete for our interest and time, but that is clearly a different matter.)

36 *Random House Unabridged Dictionary*, 2nd ed., ed. in chief Stuart Berg Flexner (New York: Random House, 1987), 998; italics in the dictionary.

37 *The Oxford English Dictionary*, 2nd ed., prepared by J.A. Simpson and E.S.C. Weiner, vol. 7 (Oxford: Clarendon Press, 1989), 1131–2. To "interpret" is said to be, among other things, "to render … words … clear or explicit," and "To make out the meaning of, explain to oneself." For the latter sense, one of the examples given is the following one from Cowper 1795: "The child who knows no better Than to interpret by the letter A story of a cock and bull" (all quotations from 1131).

38 What is called interpretation in the following citation from Gillian Brown, *Speakers, Listeners and Communication: Explorations in Discourse Analysis* (Cambridge: Cambridge University Press, 1995), 23, is reasonably an instance of what I call reconstruction: "As language use moves away from short exchanges which relate to the here-and-now, towards more abstract and complex genres, the opportunities for misunderstanding multiply, and there is room for a wider range of justifiable *interpretations*, any one of which may be adequate for the listener's current purposes" (my italics). A similar use of the term can be found in a literary and scholarly context in Wendell V. Harris, *Interpretive Acts: In Search of Meaning* (Oxford: Clarendon Press, 1988), 48: "And of course just as one builds up an *interpretation*

of the total intention and qualities of each character as one progresses through the play or novel, one also builds up an *interpretation* of the total intention and qualities of the author" (my italics).

39 Matthew Kieran, "In Defence of Critical Pluralism," *British Journal of Aesthetics* 36 (1996): 250.

40 Aleida Assmann, "Im Dickicht der Zeichen: Hodegetik – Hermeneutik – Dekonstruktion," *Deutsche Vierteljahrsschrift für Literaturwissenschaft und Geistesgeschichte* 70 (1996): 548. In the rest of the paragraph, references to Assmann's article are given in the text. The quotation from p. 535 comes from Assmann's summary in English, while the other quotations are my own translations of her German text.

3

The Tree of Interpretation

Göran Rossholm

1. TO INTERPRET

Webster's dictionary divides the entry of "to interpret" into three sections:

1. To explain the meaning of; to expound; to translate, as from an unknown or foreign language into one's own; to explain or unfold the intent, meaning, or reasons of; to make clear; to free from obscurity or mystery; to make intelligible; to decipher; as to *interpret* the French language to an American; to *interpret* a dream; to *interpret* a passage of the Scripture.

2. To represent artistically; to portray or make clear by representation; as, an actor *interprets* a character in a drama; a musician *interprets* a piece of music.

3. To assume the meaning of; to explain to oneself; to construe; as, his statement was not correctly *interpreted*.

In the first sense the obscurity of the object is emphasized. That which is interpreted is something whose content, meaning, or whatever is not given. In the second sense the object is a work of art, and, I assume, a presupposition is that the object may be interpreted in several different ways – an interpretation of a piece of music is not just any playing of the notes in the right order. In the third sense interpretation may be mute; it is a sense close to understanding, and again, as is seen from the example, the possibility of several interpretations is suggested. According to the third example, interpretations may be true or false (or correct or incorrect), and this also seems to be the case in the first but not in the second sense. On the one hand the different meanings are united by common bonds, and on the other they seem to lack internal unity, as is seen from the array of explications of the first sense, and from the elasticity of its key notion. What is given and what is not in an experience, what is obscure and what is clear? Is an animal's recognition of food an interpretation? If an interpretation clarifies all that has struck us as unclear in Milton's *Paradise Lost*, is it then no longer an interpretation?

Against the background of the width of the terms "interpret" and "interpretation," I will take a generous stance, and try to formulate a sense with several specifications which, I believe, will welcome any acceptable – and probably to many people's minds, some unacceptable – uses of "interpret" and "interpretation." Consequently, not only paradigmatic instances of literary interpretation, such as Ernest Jones's Freudian interpretation of *Hamlet*, [1] but also the following uses of "interpret" are within the scope of my concept: Herbert von Karajan interprets Johann Strauss's *Kaiserwalzer* (by conducting it); John Gielgud interprets the character of Richard III (by playing the role Richard III).

There is, however, one distinction hinted at in the dictionary which I believe to be unbridgeable: articulated interpretation versus receptive, unexpressed interpretation. These two concepts are juxtaposed. Of course, in many cases the production is an expression of a prior reception.[2] But other cases are different: the reception – how someone takes something – may be a consequence of the production, or the reception and the production may be inseparable in time and content. John Gielgud may have had other ideas about Richard III before he acted the role than he had after, and a musician may play a score which he has never seen before he starts to play. And it is not even necessary that there is a reception matching the production at any time. The performance of a play constitutes an interpretation of the play, but this interpretation can diverge from each of the conceptions which each of the members – actors, director, decorator, and so on – has had before the performance, during the performance, and afterwards. The same holds for many other kinds of interpretation outside such work-performance cases. The interpretation by a literary critic normally grows out of the labour of producing an interpretation, and what was there at the start is often happily forgotten. And it may well be that the critic never has a global reading experience which matches what is expressed by his written interpretation.

Productive and receptive interpretations are parallel concepts: a distinction made in one will have a counterpart in the other. Thus,

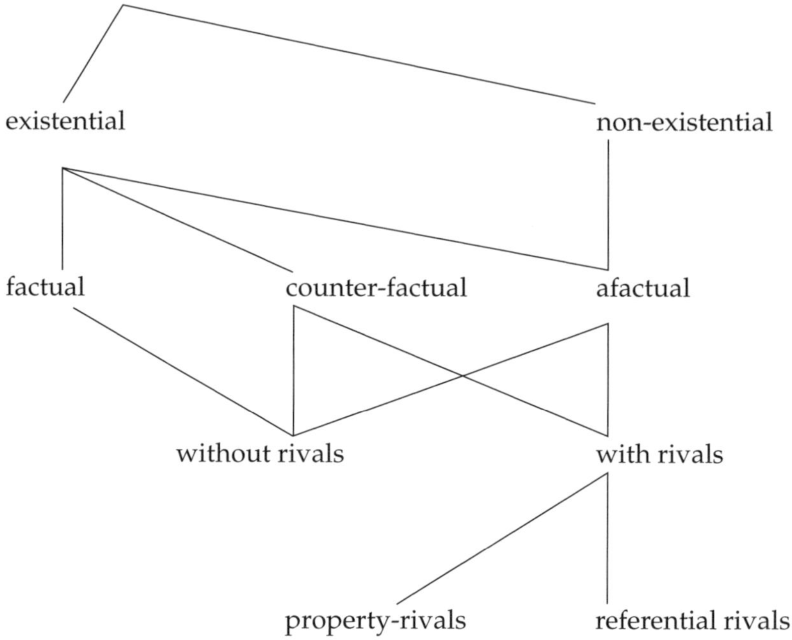

Figure 1

when I speak about interpretation in general without contextual clues pointing in any one direction, I am referring to both. [3]

The purpose of this article is to sketch what I consider the major ramifications of such a broad concept of interpretation. This will result in two hierarchical groupings of features of interpretation, graphically summed up in figure 1 and figure 2. In the context of this volume some branches are more pertinent: those leading to typical interpretations of works of art, interpretations which go beyond indisputable fact, and which are often difficult and sometimes impossible to validate, and which may conflict with another equally well (or ill) motivated interpretation. I will call such interpretations "qualified," and I will try to contribute to answering the question of how to construe a non-trivial concept of "rivalling interpretations," and also to the much-debated questions about truth and interpretation. Two of the themes suggested by the explication in Webster's dictionary will be critically discussed in this connection: meaning, and obscurity. They are both troublesome: "meaning" cries out for a theory, and "obscurity" is – obscure. Thus, I will try to systematize the concept of interpretation as far as possible without appealing to them.

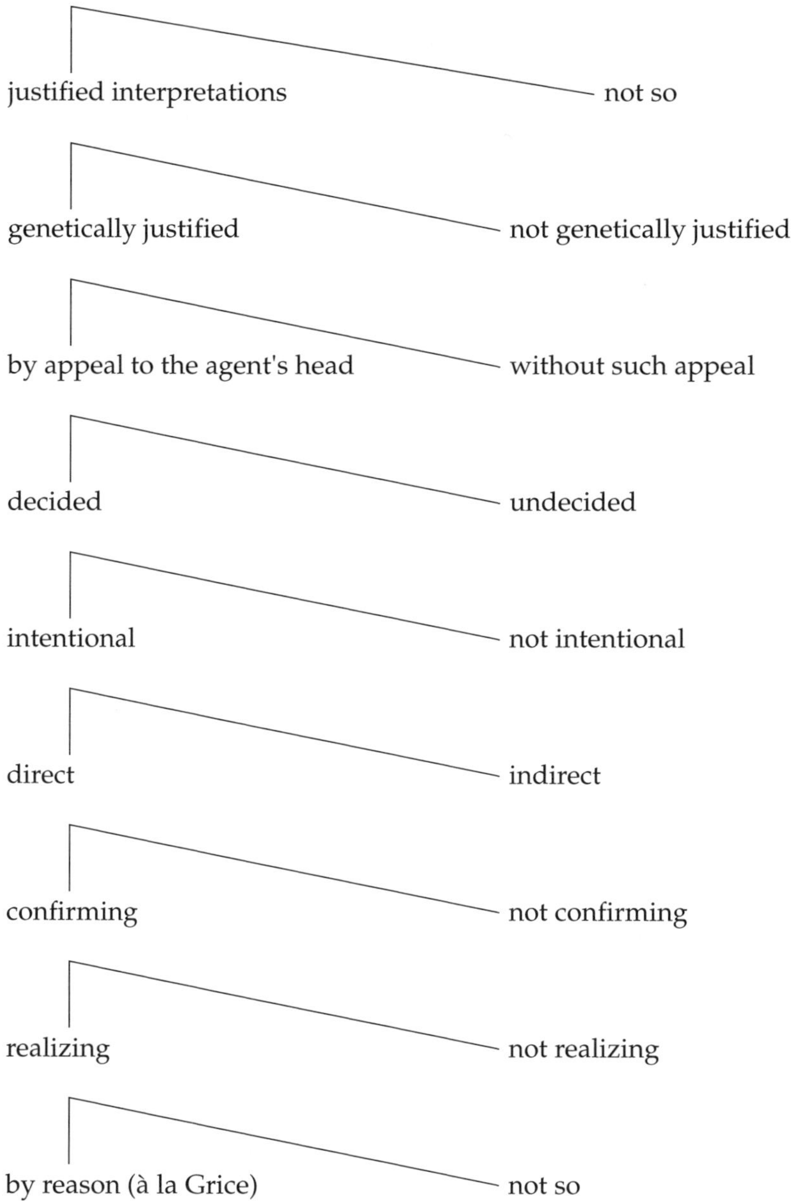
justified interpretations
not so
genetically justified
not genetically justified
by appeal to the agent's head
without such appeal
decided
undecided
intentional
not intentional
direct
indirect
confirming
not confirming
realizing
not realizing
by reason (à la Grice)
not so

Figure 2

I will also discuss the concept of intention with respect to interpretation: what "intentional interpretation" could be taken to mean, and what roles the author's intention may play in interpretation. However, I will not contribute to the lively discussion about whether interpretations should be intentional or not, or whether they are intentional or not on closer inspection.

I have chosen a subjective perspective on interpretation in the sense that I focus more on the questions of whether the interpreter takes his interpretation to be true or not, and whether he claims that it is true or not, than on the question of whether the interpretation is actually true or not. But since I presuppose that the interpreter is rational, this subjective perspective comes pretty close to an objective discussion of the same matters.

It goes without saying that such vast and complex topics cannot be treated in detail within the scope of an essay. Among the major omissions is the treatment of indirect intentional interpretation, that is, an interpretation arrived at via assumptions about the agent's intentions and some other statements. In this article this important concept is only mentioned incidentally a few times.

2. EXISTENTIALITY AND FACTUALITY

To make the root of the tree of interpretation as wide as possible we might call it an x-conception – articulated or not – not even implying the existence of x. I can have an impression of a light in the distance – my interpretation is an x-conception – without having any idea about its source; whether the light is close or at a distance, or if there is any light out there at all. I can have such an impression, and I might express having it. And I will not quarrel with anyone who claims that this is not an interpretation at all.

Any reception – seeing, hearing, or some more composite reception – may be either existential or not, that is, the recipient may take x to exist or not. And any interpretative production may claim that x exists or not. I suggest that we can choose "x as Y" to be the canonical form of this interpretative nucleus: I see/hear/read … x as Y, or I describe/present/depict … x as Y. Interpretations of art are existential when they are about the work. However, they may be phrased in a non-existential way when they are about fictive persons or events, as in "I conceive of Hamlet as plagued by his Oedipus complex."

The existential interpretation is so far neutral as to the question of the truth of the statement "x *is* Y." I will reserve the term "factual" to cover such receptive cases where the recipient believes that x is Y, and this belief is part of his experience, and such productive cases where the producer by his interpretive utterance claims that x is Y.[4] An alternative to factuality is counter-factuality: the recipient believes that x is not Y and the producer claims that this is the truth. Thus, both factuality and counter-factuality presuppose existentiality. Finally, we have the third alternative: the interpretation is neither factual nor counter-factual; let us call it afactual. Iconic reception is phrased counter-factually when I express my experience of a dog picture, x, by the statement "I see x as a dog." If I say "I see x as a dog picture" I speak factually.

The example "I conceive of Hamlet as plagued by the Oedipus complex" should be sorted under the label non-existential and, hence, also under afactual. But what if the interpreter insists that he states something true? If he does so, he is probably making claims about the play *Hamlet*, not the non-existent prince. His statement might be reformulated in accordance with Nelson Goodman's recommendations: the Prince Hamlet-renderings in the play *Hamlet* are conceived by the interpreter as plagued by the Oedipus complex-renderings.[5]

Many uses of "interpretation" with respect to works of art are existential and afactual. When a director makes a comic production of *The Cherry Orchard* – that is, he presents the play as comic – he makes no claims to the truth or falsity of the statement "*The Cherry Orchard* is comic."

Are all existential and afactual interpretations of the performance type exemplified above – playing or directing music, producing plays, and so on? I do not think so. If we rephrase our Hamlet example to be about the existing work *Hamlet*, not about the non-existent person of the same name, I think we have an interpretation of the same category. Ernest Jones interprets the play *Hamlet* in the light of the Freudian concept of the Oedipus complex. Prince Hamlet feels that his uncle has realized Hamlet's own repressed double wish – to kill his father and to marry his mother. The uncle thereby incorporates the two arch-rivals of Hamlet's inner universe, the Father (by being the real father's brother, by being the King and by being Hamlet's mother's husband) and the Oedipal wish (by being a close male relative to Hamlet's real father and by killing the real father, and by becoming the king and the husband of the mother). This experience results in an Oedipal short-circuit, which explains Hamlet's inability to act rashly and decisively. What does it mean to claim that this interpretation is true or, for that matter, false? The interpreter might argue in favour of the Oedipal interpretation in several ways, for example by claiming that

(a) if anyone behaved and reacted like Hamlet then that person would certainly be a victim of an unsolved Oedipus complex

is true, or by claiming that

(b) Shakespeare intended *Hamlet* to be about the Oedipus complex

is true. Or he might demonstrate that

(c) *Hamlet* is readable as play about the Oedipus complex.

But in doing any of these things he advocates the correctness of some statement other than the one we are considering, i.e.,

(d) *Hamlet* is about the Oedipus complex.

It should be stressed that an interpretation of *Hamlet* as so-and-so is different from the statement that it is possible to read *Hamlet* as so-and-so in about the same way as a theatre performance differs from a statement that it is possible to produce the play in that way. In both cases the interpretation does not formally imply the statement but it *shows* that the statement is true. The term "performance" could even be extended to include certain reading interpretations: the interpreter performs a reading of a work through his words.

3. RIVAL INTERPRETATIONS

It is an often stated hermeneutic saying that there is always more than one acceptable interpretation. However, not every alternative is irreconcilable with a given reception or its matching production. Different interpretations of a single work may be added to each other into a more comprehensive interpretation. If alternativeness means more than the truism that anything might correctly be described in several ways, then the alternative interpretations should be rivals, impossible to combine.

If I perceive an empty beer can as a thin tin construction, and afterwards succeed in perceiving it as solid, then I have accomplished two successive irreconcilable interpretations, one factual and one counter-factual. In this wide sense any interpretation probably has a rival. Thus, to avoid triviality, our next step should be the recognition of those interpretations which have rivals *of the same category*, and those which do not have rivals of the same category.

It is obvious that counter-factual interpretations and afactual interpretations often have rivals of the same category. I can perceive of the can as being of solid bronze and, in the next moment, as being made of paper, knowing that it is neither. I can conceive of Hamlet as a prince tortured by his Oedipus complex, and I can conceive of him as not being so.

Are there non-combinable factual interpretations? I can see a person as, factually, smiling kindly, and, in the next moment, as smiling maliciously (still factually), without any change occurring in the smiling person. I can oscillate between two rival hypotheses, favouring each as true as long as I focus on it (or perhaps the opposite). However, in order to settle this question and discuss others related to it, I will present three examples. They should all be taken to indicate non-combinable interpretations, not simply different ones:

(a) The duck-rabbit picture can be seen as a duck picture and as a rabbit picture.
(b) The Necker cube picture can be seen as a picture of a cube from below and as a picture of a cube from above.
(c) Two words in a text can be read as rhyming but also as not rhyming in the language to which the text belongs.

The two classics (a) and (b) are paradigmatic in this respect: you can see the picture as a rabbit picture (or as a rabbit) and you can see it as a duck picture (or as a duck) but not simultaneously, and the same for the Necker cube – you can see it as a cube from below, and from above. Thus the two interpretations seem to be visually non-combinable. But the same could be said about (c), where eyesight is irrelevant. And interpretations in the productive sense may also be non-combinable: you can't play the Kaiserwaltz in the manner of von Karajan – heavy, symphonic, structured in large segments – *and* as a smooth, light waltz simultaneously. So the non-combinability must be accounted for in more general terms.

One possibility is to appeal to the concept of logical inconsistency. When a word is used ambiguously in a pun, then the word simultaneously has two distinct meanings. If these are extensionally exclusive we have a word which cannot refer simultaneously in both ways. Something similar could be said about the duck-rabbit picture – nothing can be both a rabbit and a duck. The picture is referentially impossible. The reported pair of interpretations in (c) seems to present something still closer to a logical contradiction. However, the case (b) is different: it does not contain any ascription of contradictory properties to the represented object. And, on closer inspection, the tension in (a) and (c) is not that of a contradictory statement either. What is contradictory is the relation between the two terms which substitute for Y in the interpretive nucleus (to perceive x as Y). The interpreter first reads x as rhyming, then as not rhyming. (We assume that the word x may be pronounced in two different and correct ways.)

The two representational cases are discussed by Israel Scheffler.[6] The duck-rabbit picture and the Necker cube are, in Scheffler's terms, cases of multiple ambiguity, that is, symbols with two (or more) distinct senses of which we should choose both (or all). He comments upon the mentioned ambiguous images:

> The oscillation between the rival interpretations in these cases is permanent, that is, rivalry is not to be resolved in favor of one or the other but rather to be domesticated – taken as part of the function of the symbol in question. The ambiguity here involves simultaneous multiplicity of meaning rather than indecision as between one meaning and another.

Scheffler argues for the view that the ambiguity of the duck-rabbit picture is due to a double classification: it is both a duck picture and rabbit picture. And the illusion of inconsistency stems from what Scheffler calls mention selection, that is, our habit and inclination to talk about and think of representations in any media in terms of what they represent or denote. Instead of saying "Now I see it as a rabbit picture" we say "Now I see it as a rabbit." And if we take this mention-selective idiom literally we get a genuine contradiction, since no duck is a rabbit. The problem with this approach is illustrated by (b): a cube may be seen from above and from below.

However, Scheffler's solution does not depend on this apparent contradiction. He analyses pictorial ambiguity in terms of double characterization: two mention-selective labels ("duck" and "rabbit") both refer to the picture, and these labels, taken in their ordinary sense, have *divergent* extensions, that is, not necessarily exclusive extensions. But in one passage Scheffler hints at another solution, which includes the idea of contradiction: "It oscillates – now appearing to accept ducks and excluding rabbits, now the reverse. For each duck and each rabbit, it says 'yes', and also 'no'." I suggest that the explanation is to be found in the presumed fact that the labelling of the symbol classes – class of duck representations and so on – is incomplete: the "no" is omitted. Our interpretations of the symbols can be specified: duck-which-is-not-a-rabbit picture, cube-seen-from-above-but-not-from-below picture, and so on. These additions are certainly not *ad hoc*; on the contrary, the exclusions, now made explicit, are important parts of our understanding and seeing and reading.

Thus, the meaning of non-combinable alternatives can now be summed up:

> the interpreter's taking of x as Y is non-combinable with the alternative interpretation, where x is taken as Z, if and only if
> (1) any attribution of Y and Z to the same object results in a logical contradiction, or
> (2) Y and Z are representation labels consisting of a prefix for what is represented (such as rabbit, duck) plus a suffix for kind of representation (such as picture, description), and when the prefixes, taken as predicates, are attributed to one and the same thing, then the result will be a logical contradiction.

The first part of the definiens applies to (c), the second part applies to (a) and (b) above.

Thus, we have two kinds of non-combinability among interpretations: referential (as in (a) and (b)) and substantial (as in (c)). The first has to do with what x, the interpreted object, refers to, and the second with what properties are ascribed to x. But non-combinability is a relation between interpretations, not a property, which is what we need for a continuation of the tree. I suggest we continue to stick to the interpreter and make the next split by asking such things as whether a certain interpreter knows about non-combinable alternatives or not, whether he can produce one or not, and whether, when confronted with something non-combinable to his own interpretation, he would judge it to be an alternative interpretation or not.

The typical experience of the duck-rabbit picture has one more feature. The interpreter sees the picture as described above, with one addition: when he is at one of the two interpretive poles and sees the object as a duck-and-not-rabbit picture he simultaneously acknowledges that the picture might also be taken in the other way. He knows that he himself shifts, he does not believe that he is at the mercy of a miracle or a hallucination. And he acknowledges that the pair of interpretations is non-combinable and *in the same category.*

This last component of the interpretation is decisive for the question raised in the section above: can factual interpretations have rivals in the relevant sense? They cannot: when I oscillate between rival factual impressions of a person, or between rival factual scientific hypotheses, I do *not* acknowledge the factuality of the previous impression or hypothesis. If both alternatives have approximately the same degree of credibility I do not oscillate; I hesitate. The truth of the hypothesis is not just out of sight – it is lost. I acknowledge that I took an interpretation to be factual a moment ago, but I do not do so *now.* The duck-picture experience is different: I acknowledge *now* that the rabbit-picture experience is an alternative in the same category as the actual one. But that category is not factuality: the duck-rabbit picture is not a duck-but-not-rabbit picture, or a rabbit-but-not-duck picture. A duck-rabbit picture is, in Scheffler's terminology, a picture which is multiple-ambiguous between being an equivocal duck picture, and an equivocal rabbit picture, but which is neither.[7]

4. HEAD AND HAT

The next task is to expand the tree in order to accommodate intentional interpretations. "Intentional" should be taken to include ideal rational intentions, less rational intentions, and phenomena that play a causal role similar to intentions – impulses, for example.

To incorporate an interpretation, which is neither true nor false in itself, into an intentional perspective means producing a new interpretation which has a truth value and which justifies the original interpretation: the fact that an interpretation accords with the author's intention might be a reason for selecting the interpretation. This does not mean that every intentional interpretation (as I use the phrase) justifies an afactual component of the interpretation. The intentional interpretation could in itself be afactual, or the partially integrated interpretation might be factual. (Such possibilities are briefly discussed in section 6 below.) However, in the tree of interpretation – that is in figure 2 – truly justifying intentional interpretations and other kinds of intentional interpretations are grouped together.

Justification can also be achieved in other ways, and the comments above apply to those ways too. One such kind of interpretive statement is reference to the contemporary audience reactions. A rather similar case is reference to tradition. An object may for centuries be interpreted as a certain kind of picture by a certain community – say, a picture of the Madonna: the picture is taken as a Madonna picture in that tradition, regardless of the painter's intentions. Still another kind of justifying interpretation is an interpretation that may be justified by appealing to certain recipients, or to most recipients, without regard to time or tradition: the work is said to have such-and-such an effect.

What I have called a justifying interpretation has one other interpretation – the one that is justified – as its proper part. An interpretation of the latter kind is *nuclear* in relation to the former kind. I will, however, also use "nuclear" about solitary interpretations, which could be integrated into justifying interpretations. Nuclear interpretations may be factual (to see a cloud as a cloud), or counter-factual (to see a cloud as a human face, and responses to a Rorschach test in terms of objects), or afactual (to see a cloud as representing a human face, and responses to a Rorschach test in terms of representation). The class of nuclear interpretations also includes performances of music and drama, and it harbours several literary interpretations with no claim of justification. Let us then continue by distinguishing between genetic interpretations – to which intentional interpretations, of course, belong – and other justifying interpretations that are constructed in the same way by integrating a nuclear interpretation into a genetic empirical context. In a genetic interpretation the justification is to be found in the source of the interpreted object, and in a non-genetic justifying interpretation it is located elsewhere. Of course, this non-genetic branch also has its divisions and subdivisions, but as we are aiming for intentional interpretation we will not follow it further. Genetic interpretations can be divided into those which call attention to the author (or, more generally, the agent) as the source of the interpreted object, and those which don't.

If we choose the author alternative, is the next step the distinction "intentional" versus "not intentional"? I believe not. If we adhere to the subjective perspective of interpretation, then we will have to admit that in many cases the genetically inclined interpreter himself is unclear as to where to locate his own interpretation. Here is one example: "the topics discussed are sometimes stronger and more interesting than the essays themselves make clear: partly this is due to the fact that these connections were not, I think, seen by me at the time at which the essays were written, and it is only in retrospect that I begin to see their number and importance." The words are those of Paul Grice, from the beginning of his "Retrospective Epilogue" to the collection of his essays published under the title *Studies in the Way of Words.* Certainly Grice does not mean that these interesting and important connections are there by lucky chance. When I read the following pages I believe some of the ideas presented are intentional, and I suppose some are indirect – consequences of an authorial intention and something else – but on the whole I am uncertain. And this uncertainty might very well match the state of the author. As interpreters we often have a very vague hypothesis about the locus of our own interpretation – that it focuses on meanings, properties, and so on which in some sense must have come out of the head, not the hat. Thus, we must make room for this undecided attitude: a choice between decided and undecided interpretations must be introduced, immediately beneath the choice between head and hat. The next distinction will be between direct and indirect interpretations.

And on the next level we have intentional interpretations.

5. INTENTIONAL INTERPRETATION

The classical view of intentions and actions is, roughly, the idea that an agent does something, A, in order to achieve something, B, and that this activity is performed against the background of (a) the agent's belief that the best way to achieve B is to do A, and (b) the agent's qualified desire to achieve B. This version of intentionality is very strong – the means chosen is, to the agent's mind, not only a good means but the best, or, at least, no other means is better. It could be specified to be still stronger, if we presuppose that the belief stated in the second premise is in harmony with everything else that the agent believes, and that the goal stated in the first premise does not conflict with any other goal which the agent desires still more, and which he believes is attainable. In reality human intentional action often violates this ideal of rationality. The means chosen are often the best under the circumstances, that is, the best the agent can find during a limited time and without too much effort; the beliefs involved often conflict with other beliefs; and the goal sometimes conflicts with other more desirable goals. However, I will not discuss how far from the extreme point of the rational ideal we may move and still be considered to be intending creatures; I will only indicate that I, in what follows, adhere to the traditional concept of intentionality but in a more relaxed version, allowing for less than ideally rational intentions.

The problem with such a broad concept of intentionality, in the present context, lies in how to separate intentions which are relevant for interpretation from intentions which are not. If Shakespeare intended in writing *Hamlet* as he did that his audience would conceive of Hamlet as whole-heartedly loving his father, this intention is certainly relevant. If he wrote the play out of a need for money, it is less so. However, I will not present any hard and fast criteria for interpretive relevance, I will only point to four kinds of intentions. The first is the author's intention that his work should be taken in a certain way. Such intentions are communicative: the agent intends that his book should be read, his music listened to, and so on, and he further intends that it should be read in such and such a way, and so on. However, such an intention is not obligatory. An author may well intend his work never to be read, yet he might still write it with intentions which are interpretively relevant. He might then write it with the intention of making it *readable* in a certain way. This second kind of intention is implied by the first: I presuppose that the writer who intends that his work should be read in such and such a way also intends that it should be readable in that way. The third kind of intention has nothing to do with any wish concerning how it should be possible to take the work, but it may still be incorporated in an interpretation of the work. Let us say that an essay on interpretation is written with the intention of clarifying certain troublesome topics for its author; or that a novel is written for autotherapeutical reasons. In these cases the author does not necessarily have any intentions concerning the impact of the finished work. If it is possible to make use of these intentions in an interpretation, they are, to my mind, interpretively relevant.

The fourth and final kind is more of a specialty: the philosopher Paul Grice's theory of intentional meaning, which during the last decades has invaded non-philosophical areas, such as linguistics, cognitive psychology, and literary theory. Grice contrasts two kinds of meaning by alluding to the classical semiotic dichotomy natural-conventional signs (the latter called by Grice "non-natural"). One example of natural meaning is this: "Herod presents Salome with the head of St John the Baptist on a charger." If Herod instead had said to Salome "John the Baptist is dead" he would have meant something non-naturally.[8]

The example does not reveal anything of Grice's originality; his comments on the two kinds of cases do. In the first case as well as in the second one, Herod intends to inform Salome about a fact – that John is dead – and in the first as well as in the second Salome may very well conclude that this is his intention. But only in the second case is the recognition of this intention crucial for the conveyance of meaning. If Salome fails to recognize Herod's intention – perhaps she thinks he is joking – she will not believe that John is dead as a result of the utterance. In the first case the head is evidence enough.

In the example, Herod's intention is to make Salome believe something, but the speaker could have other kinds of aims. The generalized version of non-natural meaning runs:

U (= utterer) means something by x =
U intends to
(1) evoke a reaction r in A (= audience)
(2) make A recognize that U intends to evoke that reaction
(3) recognize that the realization of (2) is a reason for A to realize (1)

Before we turn to the types of interpretation which match these four kinds of intention, we have to make two distinctions: first, between interpretations about clear-cut intentions and interpretations about other mental causes, and second, between direct and indirect interpretation, the latter mixing intentional assumptions with other statements.

Next we have to choose between *confirming* intentional interpretation and other kinds of direct intentional interpretations. The former has the form

(a) A reads x as intended to be readable as Y, and A reads x as Y

Another kind of incorporation mentioned above is *realization*: the interpretation realizes the agent's intention:

(b) A reads x as intended to be read as Y, and A reads x as Y

The expression of confirmation and realization is the second part of each. The first part contains the interpreter's recognition of the author's intention.

Neither the intention of writing an article to get clear about some problem nor the intention of writing a novel to diminish one's anguish can be met by confirming or realizing interpretations. Nevertheless, assumptions about these intentions can be interpretively fruitful. A reading based on such intentions takes the text as *the result of the way it was written*:

(c) A reads x as the result of the intention of diminishing the agent's anguish

However, the reader may focus on the same intentions in other ways, for example by projecting a process of writing into his own process of reading:

(d) A reads x as written with the intention of diminishing the agent's anguish; and A experiences his reading of x as a witnessing of the process of the agent's struggle against his anguish

Such interpretive statements as (d) are examples of indirect interpretation of a special kind. They are grounded in a reading which so to speak dramatizes the act of reading. Instead of experiencing this act for what it is – that is, as an act of reading what the reader actually reads – the reader experiences the receptive act as reading something else, or as listening to a voice, or as witnessing a scene, and so on. In this case the reader may choose to experience his reading as witnessing the process of formulation (in writing, speech, thought, or neutral) of the successive sentences of the text, and of the emotions, motives, and whatever accompanies this process. To do so is to interpret; the interpretation is counter-factual. From the propositional counterpart of this interpretation and the (assumed) intention of the author an interpretation such as the second part of (d) follows. Thus, indirect intentional interpretation may have several distinct grounds: one intention in combination with other intentions, with factual truths, or, as in this case, with other interpretations.

How do instances of Grice's non-natural meaning fit in? Grice presents many versions of the analysis, and in several of these what at first seems to be the candidate for the role of nuclear interpretation is no interpretation at all. For example, imperatives are analysed as something done with (1) the intention of making the audience do something, and (2) the intention of getting the audience to recognize the first intention, and (3) for this reason (or partly for this reason) execute the action in question. Actions, such as shutting or opening doors, are certainly not interpretations. On the other hand, the general Gricean scheme may be applied to other kinds of utterances (including works of art) than those focused on by Grice, that is, assertions and exhortations. The interpretation (b) above, which exemplifies a realizing intentional interpretation, may be an adequate response to a Gricean intention if the first clause captures a reason for the realization of the second one. It may, but does not have to: the agent does not have to have the proper higher intention, and the interpreter does not necessarily have to assume that the agent has any such intention. We must add

(e) A reads x as intended to be read in the manner of (b)

The ultimate intention – the lowest intention – is, in most versions of Grice's theory, not about interpretations, but other things, such as actions or beliefs. But by restricting interpretation to the higher levels Grice's analysis of assertions and exhortations can be rephrased, from the addressee's point of view:

(f) A takes the agent as intending A to believe that p; A further takes the agent as intending this to be recognized by A; A finally takes his own recognition of the lower intention as a reason to believe that p
(g) A takes the agent as intending A to do something, B; A further takes the agent as intending this to be recognized by A; A finally takes his own recognition of the lower intention as a reason to do B

One difference between Gricean interpretations of ordinary utterances – that is, (f), and (g) – and the rest is that the former are about the agent; the latter, including typical aesthetic interpretations, are about the symbol.

6. THE NEXUS

The kinds of nuclear interpretations and the kinds of justifying interpretations are summed up in figure 1 and figure 2. It may seem natural to attach the network of figure 2 to the branches of figure 1. Every nuclear interpretation, factual, counter-factual, or afactual, with or without rivals – substantial or referential – could be classified as embedded in a justifying context or not, and the former could be classified as embedded in a genetic context or not, and so on. However, the interpretive embedding statements have the same form as the nuclear ones. A confirming intentional interpretation is formulated

(a) A experiences x as intended to be read/readable as Y,

that is, as an instance of the pattern "A experiences x as Y," where "Y" substitutes for everything appearing to the right of "as" in (a). Thus, the choices indicated in figure 1 should apply to interpretations of the second tree – they may have truth-value or not, they may be factual, counter-factual, or afactual, and they may or may not have non-combinable alternatives of different kinds. Intentional interpretation may be afactual or counter-factual (and so on). According to this view the structure of figure 1 should be attached to the endings of the branches in figure 2.

The resulting interpretations could then once again become integrated into more complex interpretations; an afactual intentional interpretation could be regarded as being in accord with a certain tradition, and so on. In this way we could continue to build the tree of interpretation as large as we want by using the figures 1 and 2.

However, on the previous pages I have only discussed *factual* complex interpretations, that is, interpretations where a nuclear interpretation is seen in a justifying perspective which the interpreter holds to be true. And only if such complex interpretations are factual do they deserve to be called justifying. Thus, the kinds of interpretation focused on in this article all grow on branches where figure 2 continues figure 1.

7. FACTUALITY AND RIVALRY ONCE AGAIN

The specification of alternatives in figure 2 gives, I think, a rather good picture of some fundamental kinds of *intentional* interpretation. If the stress is moved to intentional *interpretation,* and the term is applied to kinds of object notorious in interpretive disputes, such as aesthetic objects, then the categories may seem to be too wide. I suggest we call interpretations in a narrower sense "qualified interpretations."[9] Obviously all the different schematic intentional interpretations in section 5 above could be supplied by qualified nuclear interpretations and in that sense become qualified.[10] The characteristics of qualified interpretation should be found, or put into, the more foundational structure of figure 1, and I will therefore return to the notions of factuality and rivalry. These notions are more intimately connected than can be seen from the earlier pages, and they are also related to the notions in sections 4 and 5 about justification, explanation, and intention.

It seems reasonable to accept the following statements to be true:

(a) The French word "truite" denotes trouts
(b) The painting *Mona Lisa* depicts a living woman

In section 2 the statement

(c) Shakespeare's tragedy *Hamlet* represents a man, Hamlet, whose inability to act adequately and rashly is due to his unsolved Oedipus complex, that is, among other things, his repressed wish to kill his father

was considered to be neither true nor false, hence, afactual. But (a), (b), and (c) are all of a kind: they are about what is referred to by a symbol.[11] Why should some such statements be regarded as having truth value and some not?

However, the same problem might appear with other kinds of statements. In most applications a statement such as

(d) x is a bowl

is, I suppose, true or false. When Don Quijote mistakes a shaving bowl for a helmet, then (d) would have been the proper thing to say. The object is occasionally used as headgear, but its owner uses it as a shaving bowl when he shaves; it is formed like a shaving bowl, and it was probably made with the intention of its being used as a shaving bowl. So: form, fitness, habit, and intention co-operate to justify the accuracy of the statement (d) in this case. But what about cases where form, fitness, habit, and intention point in different directions? If x is produced with a bowl-intention and is never used as a bowl but as a helmet, or when it is produced to be a helmet but is constantly used as a bowl? And if it is made by an agent in a bowl-less culture with no practical intention at all, but it is made as an imitation of a bowl? Has the agent unbeknownst to himself made a bowl? And when it is produced with a clear bowl-intention, but the intention is so poorly carried out that it cannot be used as a bowl? (Everything falls out of it.) Or, let us say, that we have a saucer-producing machine, which suddenly fails and starts to produce objects which looks like plastic bowls. Which are bowls and which not?

Neither bowls nor the word "bowl" are prepared to answer all such questions. We have to accept that sometimes our bowl insecurity may be incurable. In other cases our insecurity stems from a lack of information. If I see a certain object at a distance, knowing nothing about it in advance, it may be impossible for me *in that situation* to settle the question. But the problem may in principle be solved by gaining more information about form, intention, and so on. The statement (d) may very well be true or false about the object, even if I do not know which.

This does not mean that an interpretation such as (d) must be afactual every time it is about a previously unknown object in circumstances where the object is not used.[12] The object may, so to speak, be so bowlish that I may confidently infer from seeing it that it has been deliberately made to be a bowl, that it may successfully be used as a bowl, that it is habitually called "bowl," and so on. The probability for each of these convictions may be rather low, but they may be summed up in a vaguer but much more probable conviction: the circumstances are such that they support the statement (d). If it also looks like a helmet (which I know it is not) this alternative interpretation does not have the proper consequences – I see it counter-factually as a helmet, and that is all.

Nor does this mean that my interpretation is free from circumstantial knowledge. I may see x, so to speak, against the background of my circumstantial knowledge about it, and consequently see it factually as a bowl.

In this latter case the circumstantial knowledge supported my confidence in the truth of (d). In the former case the roles were reversed: I concluded from seeing x that some circumstantial bowl-statement must be true. But in both cases the circumstances, or the inferred convictions about the circumstances, are relevant for the factual interpretation of x as a bowl.

I believe that exactly the same reasoning applies to symbols such as (a)–(c) above. When I look at the *Mona Lisa* I already know or I infer that Leonardo da Vinci intended to make a living-woman picture, or that the picture is most often regarded as a living-woman picture, or that most people would see it as living-woman picture, and so on. With a little effort I can see the painting as a dead-stuffed-woman picture, but I do not hold the required supporting circumstantial evidence to be true.

What about Hamlet? Ernest Jones believed that the circumstantial evidence supports the statement (c).[13] And it is the interpreter's convictions which count. But there is a difference between this and the *Mona Lisa* case. Hamlet always speaks well of his father. If we are to believe what Hamlet says, then he loved and adored him. Of course, there is a Freudian reply to this: Hamlet idealized his father in order to repress and conceal his wish to kill him. And he also loved him, so to speak, on another level. But the problem remains. Hamlet's explicit descriptions of his father may be used in an alternative interpretation: Hamlet loved and adored his father altogether, without any conflicting, unconscious feelings or wishes. And certainly, the text does not rule out either of these interpretations. And we may form the alternative hypothesis, that Shakespeare consciously intended to portray Hamlet as unequivocally loving his father, but unconsciously he portrayed a man in an Oedipal trap. Thus, two non-combinable interpretations are both circumstantially supported, and this disqualifies Jones's interpretation from being factual. To put it generally:

If A's interpretation of x as Y is factual, then the following is true:
if X is non-combinable with Y, and A can take x as X, then A has better reasons to hold the hypothesis true that there is evidence which supports "x is Y" than he has for holding the hypothesis true that there is evidence which equally strongly supports "x is X."

However, the evidence in the examples above looks very much like that which we find in the justifying branches: ideal and less than ideal intentions, impulses, habits, tradition, effect on interpreters, and so on. The problem can be stated: Why is this kind of information allowed to be relevant in the justification of (a) and (b) but not of (c)? The answer is given in the necessary condition for factuality above: Jones's interpretation does not preclude non-combinable alternatives with as much support as his own. This leaves us with another question: If in the examples with the bowl and the *Mona Lisa* the same kind of assumptions are made to settle the question of factuality and of justifying location, does this not mean that in certain cases factuality presupposes that the interpretation is intentional, or indirect, or placed at some other of the endings in the justifying branch?

No, not really. The hypothesis concerning supporting evidence is much vaguer than most localizations. It is enough that I believe that there is some such evidence. I do not have to believe that the bowl is made with a certain intention specifically, or that it is used in a certain way specifically. However, as mentioned (section 4), the genetic interpretation may also be very vague: an interpreter may claim that his interpretation accords with what has come out of the author's head, not his hat, but disregards further distinctions. The ground for factuality is, however, still wider: a picture may count as being a Madonna picture by being so used, and this possibility belongs to the possible evidence for factuality.

Nevertheless, on principle it is possible that the evidence required for factuality could in a particular case be identical with one suited for the justifying branch. In that case an interpreter would present an interpretation with two distinct places of residence, it seems, and this would violate our sense of systematics. However, if a statement "x is Y" was such that to be true it demanded, for example, that the statement "x is produced with the intention I" was also true, then the statement "x is Y because it is produced with the intention I" – the presumed candidate for the justifying branch – would lose its justifying force. The intention-statement and the attribution of Y to x would be too closely knit.[14] If the interpreter would like to add an explanation he would be obliged to choose something else.

At the beginning of this section I used the concept of qualified interpretation; I would now suggest that a qualified interpretation is afactual, and that it has rivals. There are, however, at least two more ideas about qualified aesthetic interpretation which ought to be discussed: the role of *meaning* in aesthetic contexts, and the obscurity of the uninterpreted object and the subsequent need for clarification.

8. MEANING

Let us once more use Jones's interpretation of *Hamlet* as an example of qualified literary interpretation. It has no truth value before it enters its genetic perspective, it is afactual, it is non-ideally intentional, it is not intentional à la Grice, and the relation between reading and intention is confirming. A reading of Voltaire's *Candide* as a criticism of a rationalistic *laissez-faire* philosophy is more ideally intentional; the rest is in accordance with Jones's interpretation. I believe many examples which most of us easily associate with the concept "literary interpretation" will fit into this pattern. (Many will also fall into the category "indirect.") But the same places will be given to interpretations such as

A reads the token x as rhyming to the token y

As in the earlier example, the word x allows for a rhyming pronunciation, but it also allows for a non-rhyming pronunciation. Thus, the interpretation lacks truth value and is afactual. It may be placed in an intentional perspective, and the intentional interpretation may confirm the rhyming reading. Thus, so far it is co-classified with the *Hamlet* or the *Candide* interpretations. The only deviation from these interpretations is that the pronunciation has only property rivals while the literary interpretations have referring rival interpretations. This is a significant difference, but it would be a simplification to demand that aesthetic interpretations consisted of nothing but statements about what is represented – depicted, described – by the work. In practice written interpretations consist of a body of statements, which, taken separately, belong to different parts of the tree of interpretation and which cohere in numerous ways, for instance by supporting each other. And some works of art are objects of interpretation in spite of their lack of reference.

One remedy could be to widen the concept "referential": not only representation but allusion, expression, variation, and a lot of aesthetically significant concepts could be included in reference by following Nelson Goodman's semiotic recommendations. Expression in locutions such as "the music expresses sorrow" is analysed as metaphorical exemplification. The label "sorrow" taken as metaphor is exemplified by the music. Literal exemplification is also a species of reference: you may play a sharp C to exemplify the label "C sharp" instead of denoting it by uttering "C sharp". Combinations of denotation and exemplification make up indirect reference: you may refer to something via a mediating sign, as is done in allusion. I am convinced that Goodman's referential theory is the most promising attempt to create a powerful and systematic semiotics.

If we – as I suggest – reinterpret the term "referential rival" in figure 1 in a Goodmanian direction, we can add to the requirements of a qualified aesthetic interpretation that it should have referential rivals.[15]

However, that does not mean that a qualified aesthetic interpretation should consist *only* of statements which are referential, even in this wide sense. Indeed, it is probably impossible to exclude any kind of statement from a valuable interpretation. The most that may be required is that the parts of an interpretation contribute to a referential account – still in the wide Goodmanian sense – which covers much of the artwork.

A rhyme may serve as example. In T.S. Eliot's *The Love Song of J. Alfred Prufrock* we can read

In the room the women come and go
Talking of Michelangelo.

A rhyme is by itself not referential. So, what difference would it make to replace Eliot's lines with the following?

In the room the women come and pass
Talking of Michelangelo

There are several differences between the two couplets. The rhyme contributes to a higher degree of unity and separateness from the rest of the poem; it invites comparisons between the rhyming units; it thereby contrasts a one-syllable word to a word of four or five syllables (depending on your pronunciation); one of the most frequent and commonplace verbs in the English language is set against the name of one of the heroes of Western culture. The rhythm in terms of number of syllables and stresses is the same in the two couplets. Yet, the rhyme emphasizes the small differences between the two lines in Eliot's poem; the discrepancy between the lines increases the comical expression of the couplet. And I would even say that the mimetic content is affected: the emptiness of the women's words is more salient in Eliot's lines than in the unrhymed ones.

We have here two options: either to follow the suggestion above and count the rhyme (or more exactly, the reader's reading of x and y as rhyming) as a part of an interpretation, or to count it as an argument for an interpretation but not in itself belonging to that interpretation. Intuitively the first way seems right. Even if an astronomer and a student of Nostradamus both predict the arrival of a comet they would probably still deeply disagree, since their ways of prediction are so different. Likewise two interpreters who came to the same conclusion with respect to the mimetic content of a certain work would seriously disagree if they reciprocally denied the validity of each other's arguments. It seems more appropriate to say that they differ in their interpretations than to say that they present one and the same interpretation.

It would also be difficult to make sense of the idea that their interpretations were identical. In the case above A would say that the rhyme contributes to a comical air while B would reply that the lines are comical in exactly the same way and to the same extent that A claims, but that the rhyme has nothing to do with it. It seems more reasonable to say that A and B disagree on the subject of the comical value of the couplet since they disagree on the subject of the role of the rhyme in this context. Argument and expressive interpretation are in this case inseparable.

9. OBSCURITY, NOVELTY, AND QUALIFIED INTERPRETATION

The delimitation made – afactual interpretations about artworks, with referential rivals – probably includes most writings which spring to the literary critic's mind when he hears the words "literary interpretation." But no explicit distinction has so far been made between dull and superficial paraphrases of a work and interpretations which surprise, solve riddles, and present the work in an unexpected light. Ernest Jones presents an image of Hamlet, and of *Hamlet,* which forcefully deviates from earlier known interpretations. And, if we return to Webster's explication of "to interpret," we can observe one semantic feature which is ignored in figure 1: "to translate, as from an unknown or foreign language into one's own; to make clear; to free from obscurity or mystery; to make intelligible; to decipher; as to *interpret* the French language to an American." What is interpreted is initially unintelligible or obscure; interpretation removes obscurity and establishes clear understanding. However, such a characterization must immediately be modified to apply to literary interpretation, which does not depend on the recognition of something obscure prior to the interpretation. There do not seem to have been many problems with Hamlet before Romanticism. And a literary interpretation may begin by pointing out obscurities not hitherto noticed. Thus, let us preliminarily say that a qualified literary interpretation clarifies obscurities recognized prior to the interpretation or presented by the interpreter.

However, if we continue this line of thought, then we might run into the conclusion that an interpretation ceases to be qualified as soon as it is understood. The deciphering of the Rosetta Stone was once a qualified interpretation, but only for a very short time. Should we say instead that an interpretation of a work is qualified, if and only if it has changed our way of receiving the work? No, this delimits the class of qualified interpretations to publicly successful qualified interpretations unless we take "us" very loosely: if *my* interpretation of work w renews *my own* conception of w, it has changed "our" way of recognizing w.

But such a formulation still has an unwelcome consequence: every first reading, however trite, becomes a qualified interpretation, since it is a new reading. And if we require a qualified interpretation to compete with an already existing interpretation, then we have the opposite unwelcome consequence: no first reading could ever be qualified.

Perhaps the fault lies in that the perspective of change and newness is too narrow: we should perhaps measure the new reading not only in relation to previous readings of the same work but also to readings of similar works. Jones's interpretation of *Hamlet* not only deviates from earlier *Hamlet* interpretations but also from most *King Lear* interpretations, *Macbeth* interpretations, *Othello* interpretations, and so on. The change and the novelty are then transferred to another level.

Such an account of qualified interpretation is, of course, very relativistic – what is new for A is old for B, and what is obscure for A is clear for B. It is also problematic in other respects. For instance, how do we select the "similar works," mentioned in the previous paragraph, and how do we make the evaluation of a given interpretation's novelty in relation to interpretations of the selected corpus?

The approach has more serious shortcomings, however, and these remain even if we state that change and novelty are only necessary conditions for qualified interpretation. It disqualifies a number of interpretations which are far from being trivial indisputable observations of features of the work. A psychoanalytical interpretation of a new – previously uninterpreted, and even unread – literary work would not deviate from interpretive practice as far as Jones's study did when it appeared. No university teacher of literature today is surprised by the discovery that a student has written a psychoanalytical paper on a literary work. And in most cases the university teacher finds nothing principally new in these approaches. According to the reasoning above, such an interpretation is not qualified for the teacher. Still, even the teacher probably holds the interpretation to be different in kind from a paraphrase.

The cause of this predicament lies, I believe, in the very beginning of this argument: to clarify what appeared incomprehensible – to decipher the Rosetta Stone – is taken as characteristic of qualified aesthetic interpretation. Of course, the interpreter of art often explicates obscure points in texts, paintings, or whatever, but such clarifications have one feature which contrasts with Jones's reading of *Hamlet*: when the deciphering is done facts are established, and not only facts about how the stone may be read but also about what it says – how it is to be read. Jones's interpretation lacks truth value and establishes no more facts; it just shows one way in which to read *Hamlet*. And I suggest that the vague concept of qualified aesthetic interpretation is already accounted for: it is an interpretation of an artwork; it is afactual, has no truth value, and has referential rivals. In these respects the student's far from original psychoanalytical interpretation is of the same sort as Jones's interpretation, and they both differ from an indisputable paraphrase. There is no need to further stress the contrast between such interpretations and trite paraphrases; the latter are usually true or false, and they lack rivals.

10. SUMMARY

Instead of presenting a notion of interpretation that is contrasted to description and analysis and also separated from interpretation as performance, I have chosen to start with a concept that includes performances and uncontroversial descriptions and analysis as well as such things as literary scholars enclose with their applications for academic posts and scholarships.

Within this wide concept there is a subclass of justifying interpretations that contain less complex interpretations as parts. This subclass is further subdivided, as is shown in figure 2. Some of the pigeonholes in that figure are only casually mentioned. In particular the heterogeneous group dubbed "justified, but not genetically" includes interpretations which are (supposed to be) justified because they conform to certain reader's reactions, or because they maximize coherence, intelligibility, or whatever. I would also like to place what is often called "hypothetical intentionalism" here.[16] The emphasis is put on the intentional part of the branch of the genetic interpretations, because of an interest in clarifying the ambiguous phrase "intentional interpretation."

The role played by the key concepts in the justifying tree is a double role with respect to truth. The justifying embedding of a nuclear interpretation without truth value may be a true interpretation, but the very phenomena focused on by the complex interpretation – in particular intention – may also be evidence for validating a nuclear interpretation. In the first case a genetic statement about the object as taken in a certain way is true – for example, the statement "This bowl is designed to function as a bowl." In the second case a statement to the effect that the object is as it is taken is true – for example, the statement "This is a bowl" – and genetic considerations may function as a reason for taking it to be true.

The central notion with respect to interpretations of artworks is rivalry, or conflict, among interpretations, and it may be summed up as follows: A rational interpreter cannot simultaneously interpret one object in two ways such that (1) he claims/believes that both are true, (2) they contradict each other.[17] Interpretations which are not held/claimed to be true can conflict, and this clash can be demonstrated as a logical contradiction between two sentences which are correlated to the interpretations. This does not mean that *the interpretations* contradict each other, only that the logical notion of contradiction is crucial in the understanding of this kind of interpretive conflict.

Finally the integration of the semiotic dimension – that artworks have meaning – is sketched. But the more diffuse claim that interpretation (of artworks in particular) must clarify what is obscure prior to the interpretation, or that an interpretation must renew the understanding of the object, is rejected. What is to be saved from these intuitions is already taken care of by the observation that the typical artwork interpretation is afactual and that it has rivals.

NOTES

1 Ernest Jones, *Hamlet and Oedipus* (London: Victor Gollancz, 1949).

2 The term "production" should be read: "external production." Reception may, of course, also have products – internal ones.

3 The distinction reception-production should not be confused with the distinction between interpretation as process and interpretation as product. A receptive interpretation, as well as a productive interpretation, first has a process phase, which may end in an interpretation-product – external or internal.

4 Göran Hermerén thinks that the formula "X interprets Y as Z" might lead to infinite regresses unless a line is drawn between interpretation and description: "we would have to assume that there is a Y' which X interprets as Y, and that there is a Y'' which X interprets as Y', and so forth." I guess that these worries rest upon two presuppositions – that the formula must be read *de dicto*, as implying that X is willing and capable of describing the interpreted object by the term "Y," and that the regress could not be

stopped by the supposition that X interprets Y as Y. I believe that interpretations are often of the latter kind – to call a stone a stone – and also that the formula could be read *de re,* not *de dicto.* Göran Hermerén, "Interpretation: Types and Criteria," in J. Margolis, ed., *The Worlds of Art and the World,* Grazer philosophische Studien 19 (Amsterdam: Rodopi, 1984).

5 See Nelson Goodman, "On Likeness of Meaning," *Problems and Projects* (Indianapolis: Hackett, 1972), and *Languages of Art: An Approach to a Theory of Symbols* (Indianapolis: Hackett, 1976), 21–6.

6 Israel Scheffler, "Pictorial Ambiguity," in *Symbolic Worlds: Art, Science, Language, Ritual* (New York: Cambridge University Press, 1997).

7 I use the duck-rabbit to illustrate the concept of rivalry. This does not mean that I take symbols made to be ambiguous to be representative of interpretable objects in general. Robert Stecker emphasizes this character of the duck-rabbit picture in his dismissal of the idea that incompatibility among interpretations should and could be grounded in the notion "seeing-as." I simply ignore the prehistory of the duck-rabbit. Furthermore, Stecker does not recognize the negative moment in the perception – I see it as a duck, *not as a rabbit*. *Art Works: Definition, Meaning, Value* (University Park: Pennsylvania State University Press, 1997), 129–31. According to Stecker, two interpretations are incompatible if and only if they contradict each other in the ordinary logical sense. I have avoided the logical term "incompatible" in order to capture a wider and, I think, more important concept of interpretive conflict. Stecker's account presupposes, in distinction to mine, that the conflicting interpretations are always statements.

8 All references are to Grice's first version of his theory, i.e., the article "Meaning," reprinted in *Studies in the Way of Words* (Cambridge, Mass.: Harvard University Press, 1989).

9 I presume that David Novitz refers to the same class of interpretations by the term "elucidatory interpretation." As his explication relies on distinctions akin to the ones I criticize in section 9, I prefer not to borrow his term. David Novitz, "Interpretation and Justification," in J. Margolis and T. Rockmore, eds., *The Philosophy of Interpretation* (Oxford: Blackwell, 1999).

10 The Gricean intentional interpretations where the agent is the interpretive object – (f) and (g) in section 5 – are less typical in aesthetic contexts.

11 "Reference" should be taken in the Goodmanian sense (see note 5): being a trout-term, a living-woman picture and a man-with-unsolved-Oedipus-complex representation.

12 Apart from the two forms of afactuality mentioned here – lack of truth value and lack of information, respectively – there is a third: when inter-

preting x as Y the interpreter does not care about the truth or falsity of the sentence "x is Y." He may very well know that it is true, but he disregards this knowledge. This third kind is left in the background in the present section.

13 Most of this evidence is presented in the chapter "The Hamlet in Shakespeare," in Jones, *Hamlet and Oedipus.*

14 If Peter Juhl is right, irony would be a case in point: an utterance is ironic only if it is intended by the utterer to be ironic. If that is correct I would not add anything to the remark "That was ironic" by saying "It was also meant to be ironic." I would only spell out what had already been stated. See Juhl, *Interpretation: An Essay in the Philosophy of Literary Criticism* (Princeton: Princeton University Press, 1980).

15 This has the consequence that the definition of non-combinable interpretations in section 3 has to be reformulated. This would, however, lead us too far into Goodmanian semiotics in this context. Instead, consult the works referred to in notes 5 and 6; Goodman, *Of Mind and Other Matters* (Cambridge, Mass.: Harvard University Press, 1984); Goodman (together with Catherine Elgin), *Reconceptions in Philosophy and Other Arts and Sciences* (London: Routledge, 1988); and Catherine Elgin, *With Reference to Reference* (Indianapolis: Hackett, 1983).

16 If this position means that the interpreter chooses the interpretation which the author would probably have intended, granted a certain evidence E and no other evidence, then the interpretation is not justified by any reference to the author's intention or anything else which has to do with the genesis of the work. The interpretation is justified by reference to what a set of preselected and isolated facts will evidence. For a critical discussion of hypothetical intentionalism and references, see Stecker's *Art Works.*

17 It goes without saying that *two* interpreters may entertain factual interpretations which cannot both be true.

4

Types of Types of Interpretation

Staffan Carlshamre

1. INTRODUCTION

It is a presupposition of this volume that there are different types of interpretation and that many problems in the theory of interpretation stem from a failure to recognize this fact.

Noting the multiplicity of types of interpretation naturally gives rise to an impulse to chart the differences and create a typology. Equipped with this, we would, hopefully, be in a better position to sort controversies into verbal and real, both among theories of interpretation (theories about different things may be different without contradicting each other) and among interpretations (interpretations belonging to different types need not conflict). Encountering two parties engaged in a bitter struggle over, for example, whether the interpretation of a text should be directed towards the intentions of its author or the reactions of its readers, we would simply point out that they were asking different but perhaps equally important questions – and everyone could go peacefully back to work.

That such a goal could actually be accomplished on a grand scale is perhaps not to be expected, but an effort in that direction might nevertheless be illuminating. So how should one go about it? And what should one expect to find?

One immediate observation is that not only are there many types of interpretation, there are many typologies of interpretation and many types of typologies as well. In this book alone, we find several, sometimes overlapping, but far from identical ways of classifying interpretations. And the same is true for the literature on the subject at large – indeed, almost everyone writing about types of interpretation seems to feel the need to start again from scratch and develop his or her own classification.

In order to situate the viewpoint to be developed here, I want to distinguish three types of classificatory approach, all of them exemplified in this volume.

The first approach is oriented towards *linguistic usage*.[1] It takes its departure from the actual use of the *word* "interpretation" and its linguistic relatives, and tries to give a succinct and informative description of that use. Torsten Pettersson's article clearly exemplifies this approach.

The second approach is based on an *empirical classification*. It takes its departure from actually occurring types of interpretation that seem significantly different, from some chosen point of view; for example, with regard to questions of intersubjective validity or criteria for justification. It then tries to characterize these types in some informative way. Most of the literature on types of interpretation takes this approach. In this volume it is well exemplified by Anders Pettersson.[2]

The third approach is the one I will be trying here; in another way it is exemplified by Göran Rossholm's article. It is oriented towards *logical space*. The focus here is on the *dimensions* of the typology, not on the classes themselves. A scheme of this kind will, for simple combinatory reasons, quickly give rise to what may seem to be blatant classificatory overkill – while the scheme generates, perhaps, hundreds of slots, maybe only a handful of them are filled with anything real. So the question naturally arises, why bother?

There are basically two answers to that question. The first is that the "overkill" is an accidental by-product of the effort to provide an informative account of the "real" classes, in terms of well-chosen dimensions. The second, and more important, answer is that it is a necessary background for posing some interesting and otherwise inaccessible questions, namely, *why* are precisely these slots filled and all the others empty?

One should expect some tension between the third approach and the other two. Because many of the classes distinguished as "types of interpretation" by the logical-space approach never actually occur, there is, naturally, no established usage of the term "interpretation" which corresponds to them. And the proponent of the scheme may, perhaps, seem to take this a little too lightly, secure in his conviction that the real question is not about words anyway. But, of course, there must be *some* reasonable relation between the scheme and normal usage, and also between the scheme and the empirically salient classes.

In the rest of this section I will first give some brief indications of the nature of the classificatory scheme that I will develop in more detail in the next few sections, and then hint at some of the questions I hope can be illuminated by application of the scheme.

My first classification will be according to the nature of the "sign" (to be interpreted) and the nature of the "meaning" (to be achieved through the interpretation). The horror quotes indicate that I am a little reluctant to use the words "sign" and "meaning" across the board in this context, and I will therefore introduce two more generic technical terms: the *manifest* and the *hidden*.

Second, I will distinguish between two layers in what is usually called an interpretation: the *reading* and the *claim*. For example, two readers might both read *Madame Bovary* as a tragic story about what must happen to finer sensibilities and romantic aspirations in the bourgeois world, while only one of them claims that this is how Flaubert intended his story to be read. Correlated with this dichotomy I will make a further distinction between the *elaboration* of a reading and the *justification* of a claim.

With this framework in place, I will go on to treat some issues concerning the truth and validity of interpretations. I discuss the role of various types of claims for various types of interpretation, and I interpret the controversy over intentionalism, in literary theory, as being about the sorts of claim that are made, and the sorts of claim that ought to be made, for different sorts of readings of literary works. I am not concerned either to defend or to attack intentionalism *per se*, but I am interested in the question of why we are sometimes more and sometimes less interested in the author's intentions, when interpreting a text (or an utterance or a picture or whatever). One central, but seldom explicitly raised, question in this context is why we should *ever* be interested in the author's intentions. I argue that in ordinary communication there are, in the main, two specific reasons for such an interest, and against this background, I speculate about possible cases in which these motives fail to apply, or apply to a lesser degree than in ordinary communication. My conclusion is that the areas where the connection between valid interpretation and authorial intention has been most vividly challenged – fictional texts, aesthetic objects generally, and philosophical texts – are, precisely, such cases.

2. THE HIDDEN AND THE MANIFEST

If we want to say something completely general about interpretation, maybe the first thing we get is this. We need a contrast between, on the one hand, what is interpreted, the object of interpretation, and, on the other hand, what is sought through the interpretation, the meaning. We picture ourselves in front of the object, asking the question: What does this mean? To get to more specific types of interpretation we must say something about what sort of thing "this" might be; what sort of thing "what" might be looking for; and perhaps what sort of relation "means" might be taken to suggest between them. I will talk about the terms of the meaning relation as the "manifest" and the "hidden," respectively.

Depending on how we specify the hidden and the manifest we will get different types of interpretation.[3] I will give a rather extensive list of such pairs, adding some comments as I go along. Here is a first group of possibilities:

Manifest	*Hidden*
mark	letter
letter sequence	word
word	concept
meaningful expression	referent
locution	illocution
literal meaning	figurative meaning
stated	presupposed
explicit	implied

All of the pairs in this first group have something to do with language and linguistic utterances. Let me start from the beginning.

To take a mark as a letter of some alphabet is clearly an act of interpretation, in a quite common sense of that word.[4] The very same spatial shape may signify different letters of different alphabets. (I think I was well into my teens before I realized the relation between the fact that the Soviet Union was abbreviated to "*SSSR*" in Swedish and the fact that Soviet hockey players had "*CCCP*" printed on their shirts.) It may be doubtful whether a piece of scribble on a sheet of paper is an example of somebody's handwriting, or just a collection of meaningless shapes, and the decipherment of it – if it is writing – may be a laborious interpretive task.[5]

On the next level, we may take some marks as signifying a determinate sequence of letters and still wonder whether they make up a word, and if so, which one. Is "rock" the term for a large stone, or for a certain musical genre, or is it the Swedish word for a man's overcoat? These are not just different meanings of the same word – they are different words composed of the same letter sequence.

Taking word identity as established, we may go on to ask about what the word means, what concept is associated with it on a particular occasion. Does the word "prince" in a certain context carry the significance of "sovereign ruler" or does it mean "son or grandson of a king or queen"?

On the next level we may go on to ask whether the linguistic expression in question, its sense taken as established, *refers* to anything and, if so, to what. Does the word "prince," in this utterance, refer to a particular person? And, if the answer is yes, who is it?

Let me stop here for two general observations. The first, and obvious, one is that interpretations of different types go together in hierarchies – what is "hidden" for one interpretation may itself be "manifest" for another interpretation, on another level of the hierarchy. And this leads to the second observation, that interpretive tasks are often underspecified – to speak of interpreting a "text" or an "utterance" often gives very little clue not only about what is taken as hidden, what is sought through the interpretation, but also about what is taken as manifest, the clue from which the investigation starts.

The particular ladder we have climbed so far obviously has some connection with the different aspects of what J.L. Austin called the "locutionary act." To perform a locutionary act is, according to Austin's account, to utter certain sounds as belonging to a certain language, with a certain grammatical structure and so forth, and with a certain intended sense and reference.[6]

Let me come back to the list. In Austin's terms, a natural next step is to take a complete locution (with its sense and reference) as the manifest, ready to be interpreted as expressing a certain illocutionary force.[7]

I will not comment on the pair literal-figurative; obviously there is a lot of variation hidden under that umbrella. To motivate the inclusion of the pair stated-presupposed I will just provide the following quotation:

> The task of an interpreter of Parmenides is to find the simplest, historically most plausible, and philosophically most comprehensible set of assumptions that imply (in a suitably loose sense) the doctrine of "being" set out in Parmenides' poem.[8]

I take this to mean that to interpret Parmenides is to supply a background of assumptions, for various reasons unstated by Parmenides, that make it reasonable or natural to say what the poem actually says.

Obviously, this type of interpretation will have to assume that lot of interpretation on other levels is already in place.

For the pair explicit-implied I will do no more than refer to Paul Grice's discussion of conversational implicature.[9]

So far, all of my hidden-manifest pairs have been, in a broad sense, "linguistic." But this is not generally so. There is a wide range of cases where the same structure is present, and where we speak, comfortably, of "interpretation," but where neither the hidden nor the manifest must necessarily belong to a language, or be related to an act of utterance. Look, for example, at this group of five:

part	whole
example...............	generalization
generalization	example
rule...................	application
application	rule

Again I will comment briefly on each pair, in turn. Theories of how we understand stories and pictures rightly emphasize our ability to "fill in" and "flesh out" what we are actually told or shown, supplying missing details and unmentioned surroundings: we reason from *parts* to *wholes*.

To take whatever is concretely told in a story as an *example* and to *generalize* it – either in a descriptive or a normative dimension – is one of the most common and striking interpretive modes, both among professional critics and laypeople. Indeed, if Aristotle is right, this is the main point of art – to express general truths about reality by means of examples that might not themselves be real.[10] All thematic interpretation – "this is a love story," "this is a story about city life in the 1990s" – is in this line of business.[11]

What about the other direction? Can finding an example to fit a generalization also be called an act of interpretation? Yes, at least sometimes – in philosophy this is one of the most frequent and cherished ways of pinning down the meaning of abstract and theoretical assertions. And, in the case of literature, one type of "particularization" that springs to mind is the bringing to bear of insights from a work on the reader's own case.[12]

With the relation between *rules* and *applications* we are still in the dimension of the general and the particular. To find clear examples we may turn to legal interpretation. Fitting the law to particular cases is the bread and butter of lawyers and judges, and extracting a general rule from previous particular decisions is one of the main tools in that process.[13]

These hidden-manifest pairs clearly go beyond the confines of linguistic interpretation. The manifest, in these cases, is not a linguistic object. For example, when Ally McBeal (of the TV series) is taken as an "icon of contemporary woman," she may in some sense be said to be a "signifier," but she certainly is not an element of language or speech, and the same thing goes for a legal case used as a precedent in a trial.

So what do these types of interpretation have to do with the interpretation of texts? The answer is that they usually stand in yet another hierarchical relation to textual interpretations belonging to the previous cluster. Although not itself linguistic, the manifest in these cases may be given or presented through linguistic means – it may be described, or otherwise denoted or referred to, in a linguistic act. But, of course, it need not be. The presentation of an example may be effected through some other signifying medium, for instance by a picture or a film. Or it may simply be given in experience.

Here is a third cluster of manifest-hidden pairs:

effect .... cause
expression.......... feeling, emotion, attitude
behaviour .... action
action.............. intention, motive
means .... ends
structure .... function

Just like those in the previous group, these pairs are non-linguistic, but in another way. With the exception of the first pair, we are now in the heartland of the *Verstehen* tribes – Dilthey and Weber territory, where linguistic behaviour is taken merely as a special case of meaningful action in general.

In this company the *effect-cause* pair may seem an unwelcome intruder. But it is fairly clear that we often, and without strain, talk about reasonings from effects to causes as interpretations. We interpret tracks and traces and clues – both as we encounter them in real life and as we find them described by factual or fictional texts – and in doing so, we simply look for some salient or contextually interesting cause of them.

The *expression-feeling* pair, in a sense, bridges the gap between simple *effect-cause* and the more intentionally charged items further down the list, and at the same time it may be conveniently used to illustrate some points with a more general scope. It may look as if I am totally disregarding one of the most important and basic distinctions in the theory of meaning – the distinction between what Paul Grice calls "natural" and "non-natural" meaning. In this case that distinction would show up as an ambiguity in the expression-emotion link: the ambiguity between an expression being a *symptom* of an emotion, and the expression being a *sign* of it.

In fact, there is a chain of cases here. At one end we have expressions taken as caused by the appropriate feelings, as completely natural symptoms for them. At the other end we have expressions used as a full-blown communicative symbols for feelings – you deliberately make an expression to tell someone how you feel, or to comment on how somebody else feels. In between, there are all sorts of other cases where you may be said to pretend or make believe that you have the relevant feelings – playfully or perhaps with an intent to deceive. But in all of those cases I want to say that it is the same hidden-manifest pair at work: to interpret the expression is to "read it" as indicating a certain feeling. The distinction between the different cases will be accounted for on another level.[14]

Before I leave this section I want to make another general observation. It seems to me that the interpretation of linguistic signs or utterances is often taken as a sort of paradigm of what interpretation is – not in the sense that one does not notice that many important forms of interpretation, for example of aesthetic works, go beyond the narrowly linguistic, but in the sense that one construes the link between the hidden and the manifest by analogy with one's favourite theory of linguistic meaning, be it conventionalist or intentionalist or whatever. And maybe this leads us in the wrong direction.

The important objects of interpretation ("the manifest") in aesthetic contexts are often people, actions, and events, or chains of actions, and events, rather than words or symbols in any narrow sense. Neither the manifest nor the hidden, in such cases, is *part* of the work, but given *through* the work (given to the spectator, that is, through other interpretations, on other levels, of what is part of the work). And we interpret them for reasonable generalization, for underlying motives, for moral lessons, and so on. Now, even if we want to call such things signs and symbols, they are certainly not *arbitrary* signs, ready to be used by communities or individuals for whatever purpose they see fit. Rather they are *motivated* symbols to be evaluated and criticized, discussed and reflected upon. I will return to the distinction between arbitrary and motivated symbols, after introducing the notions of a *reading* and a *claim*.

3. READING AND CLAIM

The kingdoms of experience,
in the precious wind they rot.
While paupers change possessions,
each one wishing for what the other has got.
The princess and the prince discuss
what's real and what is not.
It doesn't matter inside the gates of Eden.

This is a stanza from Bob Dylan's "Gates of Eden." What is it about? I read it as a statement of the basic *credo* of Husserlian phenomenology – a denunciation in no uncertain terms of traditional ways of doing philosophy, as Husserl saw them, and a glimpse into the promised land of phenomenological investigation.

Let me elaborate a little on that. "The kingdoms of experience" are the realms to be opened up by the phenomenological reduction, *die Sachen* towards which the supreme principle of the phenomenological method urges us to turn. Now these realms are rotting because those who should guard and harvest them are busy with other things, blind to the riches that lie ready to hand.

The paupers, of course, are the traditional philosophers of different schools, engaging in endless discussions where all the arguments are known in advance, and everyone already knows all the strengths and weaknesses of each position.

The princess and the prince are modern science and modern philosophy, heirs to the "Queen of the Sciences," the philosophy of the Middle Ages, and ultimately of the Greeks – a philosophy which aspired to give a unified picture of man and the world. We moderns have no "Kosmos," no unified framework in which to view ourselves, the world, and our knowledge of it. Science and the different schools of philosophy give us contrasting and conflicting views of reality, each trying to depreciate what the others take to be ultimately real to the status of fiction or illusion. Phenomenology, through the *epochē*, wants to end all that: "It doesn't matter inside the gates of Eden."

Now, is this a reasonable reading? Can it be justified in any way? No, it cannot – not because there is anything wrong with it, but only because so far there is nothing to be justified. I have only *presented* a reading, I have made no sort of cognitive or evaluative or prescriptive *claim* on its behalf. Where there is no claim, the question of justification does not arise.

A typical sort of interpretive claim, on behalf of a reading, would be that it corresponds to the author's intentions. That sort of "biographical" claim can itself be made more precise in many ways. Is this the way Dylan expected his real audience to read his stanza? Is this a way that he expected some smaller elite audience to read it? Is it a reading that he foresaw as possible, without specifically intending it? Perhaps it was put there as a sort of private joke? Maybe he just did not care whether the audience would be able to make out what the lines meant – after all, meaning is not always such an important thing in a song – but still this is what they meant to him.

One might also, of course, imagine more radically different sorts of claim on behalf of a reading. There may be reader-oriented claims – for example, claims about how the stanza *is actually read* by some more or less specific group of readers, or about how it *would be read* in some possible, but perhaps never realized, circumstances. There might be normative or evaluative claims – for example, that a certain reading makes the text *true* or *interesting* or perhaps *good, fruitful,* or *rewarding,* in relation to some explicit or implicit evaluative norm.

And, of course, for each such positive claim there is the possible counter-claim, also on behalf of the same reading, that this is *not* how Dylan intended his stanza to be read, etc. Clearly, there can be no question of justifying the reading before some claim is made; the type of justification relevant will depend on the specific nature of the claim.

But have I not already, without putting forward any claim, done some of the things that would usually count as attempts to justify an interpretation? After describing my reading in general terms I went through the stanza, attempting to show how the reading made sense of details of the text. Is that not justification? Is this not, precisely, the hermeneutic circle, which supposedly plays such an important role in the justification of interpretation?

The point is not to quarrel about words here, of course, but I want to distinguish between the *justification* of a claim and the *elaboration* of a reading. Spelling out the details of how the reading relates to the text is not to justify it, but only to present it more closely. The function of the elaboration is twofold. First, it gives more information about the content of the reading. And, second, it relates the reading to the text – showing it to be a way to read *this* text.[15]

Now, one might perhaps readily agree that this is not sufficient to justify any particular interpretive claim, but is it not a necessary *part* of the justification of any and every claim – so that the elaboration would be a part of any and every justification? I think not. In spite of what is often said, there is no general rule that interpretations must make sense of all the details of the text. A ready example is allegorical reading, which very often leaves much of what is present on the "literal" level without a figurative counterpart. The slack must not be too great, of course, or the reading will lose its interest as a reading of *this* text, but the whole thing is very much a question of degree. And exactly what degree of detail should be desired of a reading depends, again, on the nature of the associated claim, and on the various factual or normative constraints that go with it.

What happens to consistency, coherence, and the like – all the virtues associated with the principle of charity or *der Vorgriff auf Vollkommenheit*? Do they belong to the reading or to the claim? Take coherence as an example. Coherence is a feature that a reading may have, but is only a *virtue* of the reading in relation to some claim. In principle, a reading may be as incoherent as you like. Coherence is either a good-making characteristic, associated with a normative claim, or a supposedly factual feature dependent upon suppositions that the author is coherent, has tried to produce a coherent text (on the relevant level), has to a reasonable extent succeeded in this, and so forth. You don't argue for a reading – you argue for a claim – but, of course, features of the reading will play a role in the argument for the claim, and so will have to be present there.

4. TYPES OF CLAIM

I hope I have made the distinction between reading and claim reasonably clear, at least for some simple examples. How, then, does this apply to ordinary cases of interpretation?

In some cases there seems to be a rather free variation of the claim with respect to a reading. Take the case of a psychoanalytical reading of a story. For post-Freudian literature such a reading may be associated with a straightforward intentionalist claim: this is how the author wanted us to read the story. For pre-Freudian texts that possibility presumably is not available, but we may have a psychoanalytically modified intentionalist claim: this is what the author subconsciously wanted to say.[16] Or the reading may be associated with a straightforward receptive claim: this is how readers (perhaps some specific group of readers) in fact read the story. Or with a psychoanalytically modified receptive claim: this is how readers subconsciously read the story, while perhaps on a conscious level taking it in some totally different way.[17] For some readings of some texts all of these options, and more, may reasonably be open; the claim may vary between readers while the reading stays the same, and while it may be perfectly clear how someone reads a story, the claim he or she makes on behalf of the reading may still be vague and unspecified.

But it is also true that readings on some levels come with "default" claims – so much so that the effort to separate reading from claim may seem contrived and artificial. Locutions such as "x means y" or "I interpret x as y" usually do both things at once: they specify a reading of x as y, and they advance a certain claim with regard to that reading. And in many (broadly) linguistic contexts the default claim seems to be intentionalist in some quite robust sense.[18]

This is most obviously true for the lowest level of the linguistic hierarchy. That a certain piece of scribble is a Latin "C" – as opposed to just being readable as a "C" – is clearly a relational fact involving the intentions of some agent. The same thing goes for a letter sequence composing a certain word, a word being used in this rather than that sense, and so on. The only serious alternative to (broadly conceived) intentionalist claims here would be claims relating readings to systems of conventions, languages and the like. But, again, the claim that a certain sign belongs to a certain language – as opposed to just being readable according to the rules of that language – must itself be explained in intentionalist terms.[19]

That intentionalist claims are so obviously the "right" ones at these levels is, I suggest, explained by the arbitrary nature of the sign. Any sequence of written marks or phonemes could in principle be used to mean anything, but precisely because of this fact there is nothing to be gained from reading it against the author's intentions – it's just too easy. Where "motivations" start to appear in the manifest-hidden relations, the intentionalist defaults are more likely to be challenged.

I will postpone discussion of the sorts of claim most relevant for aesthetic interpretation for a while yet, but only notice in passing that it is a common, though by no means universally shared, view that aesthetic or fictional interpretation introduces some kind of modification to at least some of the default intentionalist claims associated with ordinary linguistic communication. There is no consensus, however, on how the modification works or how it should work. Some prefer some variant of "hypothetical intentionalism": the relevant claim being that the relevant reading *would* have been intended by some person in relevant respects similar to the actual author – the relevant respects including, for example, the (rough) time and (rough) place of utterance – but possibly dissimilar to the actual author in other, more "idiosyncratic," ways. As there is no guarantee that the hypothetical author, being a "pruned" version of the actual author, should suffice to narrow down the range of permissible readings to a desirable degree, one might want to add the supplementary claim that the relevant reading is the "best" one compatible with the hypothetical intentions condition. The more severe the pruning involved in shaping the hypothetical author, the larger the scope for the normative criterion will be, and there is ample space here for disagreement over details.

Let us look at another of the hidden-manifest pairs: effect-cause. The legendary Swedish police investigator Otto Wendel describes in his memoirs the puzzling case of a dead man lying in front of an armchair, with his hands under the lower part of his body. Why was it puzzling? There seemed to be only two possibilities. Either the man had been alive when he fell to the floor – but then he should have tried to stop the fall with his hands, and they should have ended up somewhere around his shoulders. Or he was already dead and pushed out of the chair – but then the arms should have been stretched out along the side of the body. After some thought, Wendel came up with the following suggestion. The man was dead when he fell to the floor, but afterwards someone lifted the body, first on one side, and then on the other, to feel for something in the trouser pockets, with the result that the hands fell into their final positions. This interpretation may be true, or it may be false, but it seems quite clear that it is one or the other. And it is clear what makes it true, if it is true, namely the chain of events actually leading up to the situation Wendel observed.

Now, it might, in principle, have happened that Wendel never gave his interpretation, but only described the circumstances, and that I came up with it myself, following the very same line of thinking. The interpretation would still have been correct under the very same circumstances. But suppose that the same description had occurred in a work of fiction. Again, the same line of reasoning might have led me to the same conclusion, or so it seems. But there is something puzzling here. Even if my interpretation in some obvious sense may be the same in the two cases, what makes it *correct* is certainly not the same. In the fictional case there is no real train of events leading up to the circumstances described – not surprisingly, as these circumstances themselves are not real. So there is a similarity and a difference to be accounted for. Again, I want to say that the *reading* of the clue remains the same, while the *claim* differs.

What claim is made by someone who offers Wendel's reading of the clue, in the fictional case? You might say, of course, that she is claiming that what Wendel thinks is true in the real world *is* true in the relevant fictional world. But that is not the point. What would make it true in the actual world to say *about* the fictional world that someone had felt in the dead man's pockets?[20] Basically, two different approaches seem to be possible. (a) The relevant claim is a *counterfactual* claim, about what *would* have been the case if what is told in the story had actually been true.[21] (b) The relevant claim is about what the author (perhaps suitably modified in the direction of the hypothetical) *intended* to be true in the fictional world.[22]

Intentionalism about fiction is often presented as a sort of extension of intentionalism with respect to ordinary utterances, the presupposition being that the default claims of fiction interpretation are, if anything, *less* intentionalistic than the claims of ordinary reading. But this kind of case shows that the interpretation of fiction may in some respects be *more* intentionalistic than its ordinary counterpart. In a factual text containing reports of incidents that may themselves be interpreted (for example, other people's utterances) we do not take the author of the embedding text as an authority with respect to the meaning of the embedded objects of interpretation. But taking the very same text as a piece of fiction necessarily introduces some new type of claim with respect to such embedded meanings: taking the road of intentionalism here means acknowledging that the author of a fiction has powers over the fictional world that authors of ordinary reports do not have concerning their subjects.

5. INTENTION AND TEXT

In the terminology of this paper much of the controversy in the theory of aesthetic interpretation turns on the question of whether intentionalist claims are, or perhaps should be, the default claims made by critics and scholars (and perhaps ordinary readers as well) on behalf of the readings they offer. There are two questions here.

(A) A descriptive question, about the *actual practice* of aesthetic interpretation. Are the default claims for important types of aesthetic interpretation intentionalist or not? Do they differ in this respect from other types of interpretation?
(B) A normative question, of whether the actual practice, whether intentionalist or not, is *reasonable* or *good?* Should it be changed in any way? Should we move away from intentionalism (as a practice) or should we move towards it? Or is it more reasonable to be liberal with respect to different types of claim? Is the whole thing just a matter of arbitrary convention?

How do we decide whether aesthetic interpretation, as it is usually practised, is intentionalist or not? One procedure is to appeal to some rules that supposedly guide the practice, and to argue that only intentionalist (or non-intentionalist) claims make it *rational* to abide by these rules. I will discuss two such rules, which often come up when intentionalism is discussed in literary theory, and which are usually supposed to count against intentionalism. I will start by just naming them, and then come back to what they are supposed to say.

(CT) The principle of the Centrality of the Text
(MI) The principle of Multiple Allowable Interpretations

Let us begin with the Centrality of the Text. I have borrowed the label from Gregory Currie, and I will also quote his characterization of the principle:

> Whatever its merits in science, realism fails in interpretation, because it fails to accommodate something that no amount of deconstructive rhetoric should have us forget: the centrality of the text. In interpretation, we make inferences to narrative intentions so as to illuminate and render coherent the text we have before us, not some text the author might have written. It is possible for an author to be moved by certain narrative intentions, but fail to give proper effect to them in her text-tokening activity: she can be wrong in thinking that enough has been said to indicate a development of plot or character, a reading made most plausible by her text may be one she fails to comprehend. When that happens (as in small ways it commonly does) the realist's path –

to infer from those diaries and other traces, the narrative intentions the author actually had – will not, by assumption of authorial error, illuminate and make coherent the text we have. The realist has ceased to be an interpreter of the work, and her intentional hypothesizing serves rather to interpret another, hypothetical work: the work that would have been written had the author's narrative intention gone well.[23]

What Currie here calls a "realist" is what others would call an "actual intentionalist," and he obviously thinks that the centrality of the text, for the actual practice of interpretation, tells against actual intentionalism as a theory of that practice. In this he is not alone, of course, and advocates of actual intentionalism usually take care to defend themselves on this point.[24]

But what does it mean to say that the "text" is "central" to interpretation? After some stage-setting, I will offer two suggestions, the second one being the more relevant for intentionalism.

A good deal depends, of course, on what the word "text" is taken to designate. What is "the text" for an interpretation? One seldom meets any very clear answers to that question. But in the present terminology several possibilities spring to mind.

(1) The text is *some designated layer* of the hidden-manifest structure – for example, one of the linguistic layers of my first group.
(2) The text is the *manifest*, the "object" to be interpreted.
(3) The text is the *whole hidden-manifest structure* below the level of the relevant reading.

Sometimes when one speaks of the "text" to be interpreted, one seems to have something narrowly linguistic (even syntactic) in mind, on the lines of (1). And, perhaps, there is a picture in the mind of many who use the word "text," in disputes over the nature of interpretation, of the text as being something absolutely concrete – what "meets the eye" – given before any interpretation is called for. But, of course, anything that serves as a basis for literary interpretation is already far removed from being just a collection of physical stains on sheets of white paper, and is already shot through with relations of different sorts – to languages, language users, referents, situations, intentions, and so on. Meaning, on all levels, is relational through and through, and when the notion of a text is taken to extremes there is simply no meaning "in" the text.

According to the explication (2) the word "text" would be a synonym of what I have called the "manifest." The type of interpretation that is Currie's primary focus in the quoted passage is "narrative interpretation," where one tries to reason from "what is said" to developments of plot or character. The relevant way to take what is "in the text" for this sort of interpretation seems to be simply as "what is said" – but what is said, in this sense, is of course not directly visible on the page, but can only be accessed by way of many logically "earlier" types of interpretation.

But if we are looking for a special sense in which the text is central to precisely *aesthetic* interpretation, the explication (3) is perhaps more promising. In most ordinary cases, the manifest is completely subservient to the hidden; it is treated only as a clue to its own "meaning." Once I have understood what you wanted to say, I no longer remember the words that you used – I may not even notice which language you spoke.

But in art this is different. The point of literature is not only to say things, but to say them *well* – and that ambition may go all the way down to the graphic or phonetic layer. Good allegory – considered as a work of art, and not as a mere rhetorical device – must be enjoyable on the literal level as well. And the colour, texture, and composition of a painting are not merely means to the end of representing something.

Perhaps it is easy to overstate this feature of aesthetic interpretation, but I think it corresponds to a widespread intuition. Following Nelson Goodman, I will speak of this phenomenon as the *repleteness* of an interpretation.[25] So we have a first specification of the principle of the Centrality of the Text:

(CTR) Aesthetic interpretation is replete.

Nevertheless, it is clear that (CTR) is not the relevant rendering of (CT) when discussing intentionalism. For one thing, there does not seem to be even a *prima facie* conflict between repleteness and intentionalism. But repleteness is not entirely without connection to what I take to be the relevant specification of (CT), and I will use a "convention" introduced by Brian Rosebury to bridge the gap.[26] Rosebury is interested in communicative utterances where the speaker for some reason has failed to shape his or her utterance so that it may plausibly be taken to convey what he or she wanted to say. There are, Rosebury thinks, genre-specific conventions about what may be done in such cases. In conversational exchange, and most other ordinary communicative situations, a "convention of supplementary explanation" comes into play. The speaker simply has the right (within limits) to supplement or change formulations afterwards, should they turn out to be infelicitous in some way. When this is done the new version replaces the defunct one, and is taken to reveal the speaker's true meaning.

But in aesthetic contexts (as well as in some other cases) this convention does not apply. The work of art is taken to be "complete" at the time it is issued, and may not be tampered with or "corrected" by the artist or anyone else.[27]

What explains this difference? It may well have to do with the "repleteness" of artworks. If the "lower" signifying levels are parts of the work in their own right, they cannot be changed without affecting the identity and the essence of the work. Rosebury does not go in this direction, however, but instead connects the convention with our second principle, the Multiplicity of Allowable Interpretations: "It is understood that a 'literary', or aesthetically closed, utterance, being insusceptible to limiting supplemental commentary by the author, may legitimately be interpreted variously, to the extent that its locutionary meanings and illocutionary force allow."[28] Here the ground has subtly shifted. There is no longer any question of possible deficiencies in the work, which the author is, so to speak, forbidden to remedy. Instead, the fact that certain supplementary *evidence* is not allowed in itself renders the meaning of the work to some extent variable or indeterminate, regardless of any question of the author wishing to "correct" herself. It is this constraint on allowable evidence that is the heart of the matter in my second specification of (CT):

(CTe) Aesthetic interpretation must not appeal to "external" evidence.

This is what the fight against "the intentional fallacy" in aesthetics is largely about – and clearly it is this that Currie has in mind in the passage quoted earlier.

I will not go into the question of what would define the border between external and internal evidence for (or against) an interpretation. Meaning is always relational, and so in a sense always external to whatever is supposed to carry it. Currie gives the standard sort of examples of external evidence – "those diaries and other traces" – and I will just grant, for the sake of the discussion, that there is some reasonable way to draw the desired distinction.

I have argued that an "interpretation," as the word is normally used, comprises a reading and a claim. One possibility, with regard to the injunction against external evidence, is that it does not concern the justification of the claim, but only the elaboration of the reading. In elaborating the reading, I point to elements of the manifest, indicating what specific role they have in revealing the hidden, how they relate to each other, and so on. By doing so I usually try to "illuminate and render coherent the text we have," and the reason we do not appeal to external evidence in this process is that we do not appeal to any evidence at all – we just try to get a reading across.

But suppose there is also an evidential constraint on the *justification* of standard interpretive claims, in aesthetic contexts. What would that tell us about the nature of the relevant claims? Does it rule out construing the default claims of literary interpretation along the lines of "realism" or actual intentionalism? Does the evidential constraint have to be inherent in the nature of the claim?

There may seem to be counter-examples, where similar constraints are imposed, arguably without any corresponding modification of the claim. Think about law courts, for example. There are laws concerning permissible evidence that in some cases seem to rule out the use of evidence clearly relevant to the question of guilt. But there are obvious reasons behind these constraints, concerning limitations on police proceedings, and so on. And it is hard to think of anything comparable in the aesthetic case.[29]

Another case for comparison is psychoanalysis. It might look as if the analyst is trying to reconstruct parts of the life history of the patient, while simultaneously forbidding herself access to almost any of the most obvious sources of relevant information: no interviewing of parents, childhood friends, or teachers, and no consultation of written sources. Instead she contents herself with the patient's own testimony, with no attempt at external corroboration or exposure of falsehoods, even where that would be quite easy. Again, one might perhaps argue that there is an external motivation for this constraint, namely, the importance of the bond of trust between analyst and patient. But in this case, there is a strong pull to reinterpret the claims advanced, so that the evidential constraint shall not be irrational. The real goal of the process would not be the reconstruction of an "objective" life history, but of something defined in more subjective terms.

And in the case of aesthetic interpretation there seems to be no plausible excuse at all for the evidential constraint if the goal of interpretation is defined in terms of the real author's real intentions. Can there be any other reasonable rule of evidence than to use everything relevant that one can lay one's hands on? So if you accept the evidential constraint as part of the practice, it seems that you should also accept a modification of interpretative claims, either in the direction of hypothetical intentionalism, or perhaps in some even more directly normative or evaluative direction.

I will be briefer with regard to the pluralistic principle (MI), though it is also very much in need of clarification. Everyone acknowledges, of course, that there may be many different interpretations of the same text – different questions yield different answers. But the principle of interpretative pluralism says something else, namely, that there may be incompatible but equally acceptable interpretations of the same text – competing but equally good answers to the same question. Now "equally good" in this context is not supposed to mean "equally good as far as we know"; it is not an epistemological quandary. We want to say that they are "equally true," and perhaps explicate that phrase in the usual manner, in terms of all *possible* evidence.

Expressing the principle in this way, we seem to have something that philosophers are used to talking about – a case of theories being underdetermined by data, or perhaps a case of the "indeterminacy of interpretation." The only unusual thing appears to be that in the case of literary interpretation this sort of underdetermination is not regarded as merely a remote, even if philosophically significant, possibility, but as an ever-present and practically important reality.

At this point it becomes obvious that the two principles are not independent of each other. If we limit the amount of possible evidence relevant to a theory, we will increase the underdetermination. And that is just what the principle of the centrality of the text does – it severely limits in advance the amount of possible evidence for or against an interpretation.

6. WHY EVER BOTHER?

Let us, for the sake of the argument, accept that intentionalist claims have, in some respects, a weaker standing in aesthetic interpretation than in many other contexts. Is there any reason for this state of affairs, or is it just an arbitrary convention that we treat artworks in this somewhat special way?

As hinted at the beginning of the paper, I want to approach that question by way of a detour. In a sense, aesthetic interpretation may seem to be an obvious winner, as far as interpretive attitudes are concerned. The only thing actual intentionalism does is to *narrow* the scope for possible interpretations, excluding readings that might have proved to be interesting, fruitful, enlightening, or fun. Why should we not always let ourselves be free? Why should we ever be interested in the author's intentions?

As far as I can see there can be two main reasons for such an interest, and I will list them here:

(a) I need to find out what the author thinks and feels about something, because I need to co-ordinate my own actions, attitudes, or opinions with his or hers, in some suitably broad sense of "co-ordinate".
(b) I want to use the author as a source of information concerning other matters, in the standard case the subject talked about. In other words, I want to take advantage of the fact that he or she is a reasonably reliable indicator of the relevant state of affairs. And, usually, it is what the other person *believes* that is the reliable indicator – his or her speech is useful in this context only when taken to indicate what he or she believes.[30]

Suppose these are the main reasons for caring about the author's intentions, apart from the case where I take a "historical" interest in them, for their own sake. I think they will be substantial enough to motivate the importance we attach to ascertaining the intended meaning in all conversational contexts, including our acceptance of the convention of supplementary explanation. But are there cases where none of these reasons hold?

The case of *fiction* would seem to be an obvious good candidate. There is no co-ordination reason, in most cases, for me to care about.[31] And there are no factual circumstances for which I need to use the author as a reliable indicator.

(On the other hand, there seems to be no other source of information regarding the fictional world than the author. So where am I without his guidance? Presumably I am assembling a fictional world by myself, with the help of clues given in the text. Which leads us to the next theme.)

Another plausible candidate would be *aesthetic* reading.[32] In the aesthetic use, an object is, so to speak, in the service of the consumer.

This does not imply that the work is consumed only for "pleasure," whatever that means. But the insight sought and gained through a work of art is not dependent on the author as an authority or a source of information. (Which leads us to the third theme.)

The third and, at least for the moment, last candidate would be texts that are expected to *stand evidentially for themselves*. You are supposed to gain enlightenment from a philosophical or a mathematical text – but you are not expected to lean on the reliability of the author for any of that enlightenment. Of course, the intended meaning of such a text may have great heuristic value; I might be quite incapable of actually inventing the argument for myself. But when I am finished with it I have made the insights my own. And trying to recreate the train of thought for myself might often be better heuristics, and lead more quickly to that goal than any amount of "historical" research.

Something similar is also true in many cases of aesthetic interpretation. It is a pleasure to read Jane Austen, Dostoyevsky, or Proust, but we expect something more from such reading as well – we expect to be a little wiser. And we expect that wisdom to come about through our reflection on the stories and their characters. But we are not prepared to accept such insights on the word of the author – though we may be quite aware of the moral he or she wants us to draw, we reserve the right to our own opinions.

NOTES

1 I will not use the term "conceptual analysis," as that term is often used for endeavours that have much looser ties to actual linguistic usage than I have in mind here – e.g., for the third type of approach that I will sketch below.

2 Other examples are furnished by Stuart Hampshire, "Types of Interpretation," in Sidney Hook, ed., *Art and Philosophy* (New York: New York University Press); Göran Hermerén, "Interpretation: Types and Criteria," in Joseph Margolis, ed., *The Worlds of Art and the World*, Grazer Philosophische Studien 19 (Amsterdam: Rodopi, 1984); Richard Shusterman, *The Object of Literary Criticism* (Würzburg: Königshausen und Neumann, 1984); or, indeed, almost any of the studies mentioned in the Introduction to this volume. In practice, the demarcation between these two approaches may be blurred: it may be a moot question whether two sorts of things are *types* of interpretation in one single sense of the word, or are interpretations in two different *meanings* of the word.

3 In other words, we will get a list of more specific interpretive questions. And we might be tempted to play a trick on "meaning" and "interpretation" which it is often useful to play on troublesome words – namely, to try to do without them. Each time we feel tempted to ask what anything means, we might demand of ourselves that we pick something more specific from the list, or else add some new specification if we are not satisfied with what is already there.

4 Nevertheless, some will probably resist this use of the word "interpretation." There is usually no interpretive process involved, but just immediate recognition; there is in most cases no room for interpretive disagreement; there is, again in most cases, no phenomenological distinction between the manifest and the hidden – we do not experience the manifest and the hidden as two connected things. These are all contrasts that "interpretation" is used to indicate in different contexts, and where the mark-letter pair seems to fall on the wrong side of the fence. On the other hand, there are cases where the opposite seems to be the case – difficult cases of decipherment, cryptology, and so on. However, terminology is not the issue here, so I will just content myself with recording my usage.

5 The same thing goes, *mutatis mutandis*, for sounds in relation to phonemes, of course, but to keep the exposition simpler I will stay with writing and visual shapes for the moment.

6 Austin distributes these functions over three sub-acts: the *phonetic*, the *phatic*, and the *rhetic* acts. *How to Do things with Words* (Oxford: Oxford University Press, 1962), 92.

7 Exactly what this means depends on how you construe the notion of illocutionary force. Austin reckoned with hundreds, and maybe thousands, of different illocutionary forces. But most of his modern followers seem to be content with some small one-digit number, a sort of pragmatical counterpart of grammatical mood.

8 Montgomery Furth, "Elements of Eleatic Ontology," in Alexander Mourelatos, ed., *The Presocratics: A Collection of Critical Essays*, rev. ed. (Princeton: Princeton University Press, 1992), 241.

9 Paul Grice "Logic and Conversation," in *Studies in the Way of Words* (Cambridge, Mass.: Harvard University Press, 1989).

10 I will not stop to elaborate on the details and the different species of this sort of interpretation. Doing so would take us in two directions: towards the epistemological notion of induction, and towards the semiotic function that Nelson Goodman calls "exemplification."

11 There is a good example of an interpretive question centred on generalization in Anders Pettersson's article in this volume. The protagonist in

Kafka's "The Judgement" has problems with his father. Should this generalize to *childhood dependencies* in general (as Anders Pettersson prefers) or more specifically to *parents* or perhaps only to *fathers* (as Hartmund Binder suggests)?

12 This is, I think, at least one aspect of what Anders Pettersson calls "assimilation." See p. 54 in this volume.

13 Here we are in a domain that many, including H.G. Gadamer, have taken as paradigmatic of hermeneutics in general.

14 Take the example of a sad expression on a painted face. I read the expression as indicating sadness on the part of the, perhaps fictional, person depicted. It seems clear that what I do, in a sense, is the same thing that I do when I notice that a friend looks sad. But I do not have to believe that the sad expression on the painting is caused by anyone actually being sad.

15 More precisely, it relates the hidden to the manifest – to what is taken as the object of interpretation, as the "given" on which the reading is based.

16 Such a claim, unlike the previous one, presupposes the truth of psychoanalytic theory, in some suitable form.

17 This would, I suppose, be a reasonable way to interpret the claims of Bruno Bettelheim, with respect to his readings of fairy tales. See *The Uses of Enchantment: The Meaning and Importance of Fairy Tales* (London: Thames and Hudson, 1976).

18 Intentionalist claims are not all of a kind, of course, and discussions of intentionalism would often benefit, I think, if they were kept more clearly apart. For some levels of linguistic communication a set of full-blown Gricean intentions seems to be relevant: where the author not only intends the receiver to read his utterance in a certain way, but also intends him or her to recognize that intention, and read it that way because of that recognition, and so on. When it comes to normative generalization, to take another kind of example, it may be true that the author intends a certain reading to be produced, but without intending the intention to be recognized (perhaps even intending it *not* to be recognized) by the reader, and absolutely without intending the recognition of the intention, should it occur, to be the cause or reason why that reading should impose itself. The story should "speak for itself."

19 Again, some may think that the sense in which I "intend" to speak or write my mother tongue, in ordinary situations, is rather weak. And I agree, but the important point is that the fact that my words are in Swedish, when I speak Swedish, is not a direct relation between the words as physical phenomena and the rules of Swedish, but mediated by facts about me and my intentions. It is often said that intentionalism must be

moderated in some way, even on the basic linguistic levels, in order to exclude "Humpty Dumpty semantics" (cf. Paisley Livingston, "Intentionalism in Aesthetics," *New Literary History* 29 [1998]: 831–46) 831, and Noël Carroll, "Interpretation and Intention," in Joseph Margolis and Tom Rockmore, eds., *The Philosophy of Interpretation* [Oxford: Blackwell, 2000], 75–6), but I think that this confuses a constraint on how it is reasonable for speakers to speak (namely, so that they will have a good chance of being understood) with a constraint limiting the application of actual intentionalism. If we really had reason to believe that some expression was used in a Humpty Dumpty fashion, in a certain text, few of us would, I think, go on to insist on a normalizing reading.

20 We're talking about the case where I, as a reader of the fiction, make an interpretive claim concerning a clue described therein – not about the case where someone *inside* the fiction ventures a hypothesis about it. Perhaps a parallel case will make this clearer. If Ophelia thinks Hamlet ironic when uttering "Get thee to a nunnery!" she makes a claim concerning Hamlet's intentions in speaking those words, the state of Hamlet's mind. But a critic who reads those words as ironic makes no claim about Hamlet's mind, because he is fully aware that Hamlet has no mind. So if anything makes his interpretation true, it must be something else.

21 This is a very rough formulation, of course, and refinements may take us in different directions. The classical reference for counterfactual analyses of fictional truth is David Lewis, "Truth in Fiction," in *Philosophical Papers*, vol. 1 (Oxford: Oxford University Press, 1983).

22 I will not discuss which of these, if either, is most likely to be the default claim of ordinary fiction reading, but only note that here we have another case of different claims being possible for the same reading.

23 Gregory Currie, "Interpretation and Objectivity," *Mind* 102 (July 1993): 418.

24 For a recent example, see Noël Carroll, "Interpretation and Intention," 77.

25 Nelson Goodman, *Languages of Art* (Indianapolis: Hackett, 1976), 230.

26 Brian Rosebury, "Irrecoverable Intentions and Literary Interpretation," *British Journal of Aesthetics* 37, no. 1 (January 1997): 15–30.

27 In some sense, Rosebury admits, revisions of artworks are allowed, but these are counted as *new* works, not as supplementary explanations and clarifications of the older work.

28 Rosebury, "Irrecoverable Intentions and Literary Interpretation," 26.

29 And even the description of the juridical case might be challenged. Perhaps it is not the business of law courts to advance claims about "who done it," but only to declare its opinion on what is proved.

30 Religious tracts are (officially) always interpreted for the author's intentions, even on levels where that interest fades for other sorts of text. The reason, I think, is that the "author" in these cases is considered to be an infallible authority on all levels.

31 The fantasy worlds used in interpersonal role-playing games would be an exception. There it is of crucial importance that you "inhabit" the "same" fictional world as your co-players.

32 I speak about aesthetic reading, rather than about aesthetic texts or objects, because it is the attitude that counts. Of course, you can query an aesthetic object for all sorts of information that has little to do with aesthetic enjoyment, and in many cases the author's intentions would be relevant for the retrieval of that information.

5

Interpreting Visual Art: Performance and Articulation

Margaretha Rossholm Lagerlöf

In the spring of 1994 I visited the Brügge museum. I looked at Jan van Eyck's *Van der Paele Madonna* from 1436. This painting aroused in me a very strong and strange feeling. My later attempts to analyse the characteristic aspects of the sensation produced the following thoughts:

– It was synaesthetic, but not in that the image symbolically referred to other senses. It was rather that the visual effect was so strong that it somehow indirectly seemed to stimulate other senses.
– The imaginary quality of the painting, its represented world, could still be sensed even very close to the painting. In fact, even right in front of the painting, the paint is still experienced both as tiny brushstrokes and as the represented world. It is hardly possible to separate the medium from its fictional dimension.
– The imaginary reality of the painting seemed visually analogous to the visible world surrounding us, but was also characteristically different. It was, for instance, perspectively different; it seemed to lack air, but it had light; it seemed to consist mainly in reflecting surfaces.
– Throughout my observation of the painting I gradually came to focus on insignificant parts of the represented world: the fold of a dress, a tile in indirect light, the hint of a shadow behind a glass window. Such elements tended to dominate in the final, overall impression.

The visual force of an image such as van Eyck's may be pervasive – indicating the functions and the potential of the image itself, maybe even the very reason for its importance in the cultural heritage. Yet it

Madonna with Canon George Van der Paele by Jan van Eyck, 1436, panel, 122.1 × 157.8 (inside frame). The Groeningemuseum, Bruges

is difficult to find a place for it within the general theoretical framework typically presupposed in descriptions of the meaning of an image. Impressions of the kind I had while looking at the painting usually vanish or are glossed over in the final proposed meaning of a scholarly interpretation.

So, how are we to deal with such aspects of a work of art? Are we to exclude them from our scholarly interest, allowing them instead to form a basis for a realm of free literary speech, or letting them remain in the silent moments of personal contemplation? There may be facets of the artwork that are very important to its visual interest and appearance, but are hard to come to grips with and account for in the discursive language of an interpretation. The impressions I gained from the van Eyck painting led me to begin an inquiry concerning the fullness of a pictorial universe, the subjective part of the beholder in the investigation of meaning, and the cognitive status of an interpretation relating to these aspects.

1. INTERPRETATION WITH OR WITHOUT SUBJECTIVE DIMENSIONS

Traditionally, there seems to be a conflict between expressing the subjective dimensions of one's encounter with a work of art, on the one hand, and giving opinions about its intersubjective meaning, on the other. I had a feeling that this was a false dichotomy, and that the reality of the epistemic situation was different, but concealed by customary models of description. My queries may be summarized as follows:

1. How can we deal with aspects of subjectivity in the interpretation of a work of art? How are reports about the impressions and feelings of the viewer, as well as formulations about the image's expression or appearance (or the expressions and appearances of elements of the image), related to discursive arguments, with claims to intersubjective validity, about the meaning of the image?
2. What is the status of the visual world of the artwork in relation to the meaning projected upon the image, in the course of the interpretation? How should we consider the visual surplus of the image, once the interpretation has sliced the visual world into meaning-carrying functions as opposed to the rest of the image (the silent parts, as it were)?

Let me describe a little more fully the traditional conflict that I want to discuss and contest. On the one hand we have a cluster of related but not synonymous terms: "rational," "discursive," and "valid." On the other hand we have a corresponding cluster containing the terms "subjective," "intuitive," and "aesthetic." I will not try to define these terms, at this stage, but I hope the reader goes along with the presupposition that there is a traditional tendency to lump them together in the indicated way.

One general way of dealing with issues about subjectivity and aesthetic enjoyment, in relation to works of art, is to separate the rational framework of scholarly interpretation from the irrational and free domain of involvement and feeling. This strategy might lead one to group aesthetic enjoyment or "application" of a work for personal or emotional effects with "performative" interpretations (like staging, acting, and playing the piano), separating them from reconstructive, intentional, or conventional analyses.

The well-meaning intention behind this kind of division would be to open up the possibility for a large variety of kinds of interpretation, without sacrificing the claim of some of them to belong, in a special way, to the domain of reason. One would be able to preserve rather strict criteria of validity for some kinds of interpretation, while at the same time admitting the pluralistic abundance of real encounters with art.[1]

When the subject of the discussion is images, this strategy of division is especially awkward, however. The significant reactions evoked by images are feelings of involvement, of "presence" within the imaginary universe, a sense of being aware of the fullness and borderlessness of pictorial devices. The aptitude of language to capture what the image conveys varies. The more general and conceptual an ascribed meaning is, the easier it is to confirm it, and the less it is about the individual shape and aura of what is shown.

There are standard ways of wiping out the personal dimension from an interpretive text, such as the use of "we" instead of "I." By this simple move the rhetoric of agreement is already established. Another way is to rely on the "normal" or the "ordinary," to justify a proposed meaning. Yet another way is to focus on the readable, the clearly conventional, the sayable in an image. Broad generalizations can harbour divergent experiences, without betraying the potentials for disagreement or scepticism.

The particular way the work of art offers itself to the viewer's gaze is easily explained as caused by the individual apparatus of her or his mind. There seem to be no secrets or problems about differences of opinion on this level. Everyone is entitled to his or her own impressions. On this level, disagreement is natural – or so it seems. On the level of discursive interpretation, on the contrary, disagreement is a challenge to the common values of reason. Nonetheless, the levels are not clearly distinguishable, but rather merge into one another. There is a tendency in recent scholarship to move away from claims of validity in interpretation to acceptance of mere "readings."[2] If such personal readings seem fruitful or powerful, if they seem to be able to persuade, they are also held to be successful.[3] But on the other hand, we still want to guard against gratuitous interpretive proposals.

Theorists working on the methodology of art history often appeal to the distinction between description and interpretation. The description must be correct in order to allow for a proper meaning in a broader sense to be established.[4] If a certain element is not a man picture there is no use discussing whether the depicted man is Bacchus or John the Baptist, or what mood he is in, or what action he is undertaking. In any case, mistakes in the description are seminal. Nevertheless, description is commonly held to relate to the level of viewing; it serves as some kind of documentation of the act of viewing.

So, a paradox arises: a subjective dimension must be recorded in a factual way. The description can be conceived as a filter for subjective impressions: only elements that are truly part of the image are allowed to be part of the description. The image is to be protected against all sorts of projections by the mind of the spectator. This protection, however, comes at a price: it avoids the particular, the nuances (yes, there is a depiction of a man in the picture, even a shouting man or a walking man, but we run into trouble when we try to talk about a man in a special mood or in colours we have no words to distinguish among). The elasticity of the description pulls the image between the general and factual on the one hand, and the particular and performative, which invites or corresponds to speculation and reaction, on the other.[5]

So much for the initial presentation of the problems I want to deal with. I will now present four cases of scholarly interpretations of van Eyck's *Van der Paele Madonna* and his *Arnolfini Portrait*. The aim is to demonstrate how subjective elements slip into the expositions of meaning. With these case-studies as background, I will then give my own view on how the subjective and the objective, the performative and the discursive are related in the interpretation of visual works of art.

2. VAN EYCK PAINTINGS INTERPRETED: FOUR CASES

The scholarship on van Eyck is wide and learned and I have only used fragments of it. The choice of examples may seem random, but it is meant to give special emphasis to my interest here: the relation between reports about the experience of viewing the image and scholarly statements about its meaning.

The texts are, of course, seldom strictly comparable; they do not cover the same sections of the material and they also incorporate connecting material in different ways. But I have looked for the effects of various approaches to the two paintings.

In the *Van der Paele Madonna* (dated 1436) the commissioner of the painting, the canon Van der Paele, is seen kneeling beside the throne of the Madonna, his hands joined in prayer; he is accompanied by his patron saint, St George, in armour. At the other side of the throne is the patron saint of the church, St Donatian, clothed in a rich bishop's chasuble.

The *Arnolfini Portrait* (1434) shows a man and a woman hand in hand; he holds her right hand in his left, while raising his right hand as if in a speech gesture; they appear in the interior of a bedroom, rich in detail (shoes, slippers, a dog, fruits on the windowsill, a *prie-dieu*, a carpet, the bed with red hangings, small sculptures with Christian subject matter); on the background wall a round mirror framed by small round images of the Passion reflects the pair and a couple of beholders, thus indicated as being in front of the scene. The man is dressed in black and is wearing a big black hat; he is identified on the basis of sixteenth-century inventories as Giovanni Arnolfini, an Italian merchant working at Brügge, and the woman dressed in green is consequently identified as Arnolfini's wife, Giovanna Cenami.

Both paintings wear texts, written in paint by van Eyck – the *Van der Paele Madonna* on the frame, and the *Arnolfini Portrait* within the painted space, as a confirmative signature beside the mirror – but these are not illusionistically incorporated into the represented world. (To me, at least, the letters do not appear to be imitating an inscription on the represented object, the wall, although scholars have described them as such.)[6]

Both pictures explicitly address the viewer by depicting him (them) in a reflection, recorded as being present in the represented world. In the *Arnolfini Portrait* this reflection is one of the main themes of the painting, while in the other picture the reflection is subdued, scarcely visible (on the shield of St George).

The obvious place for me to start is with Erwin Panofsky's *Early Netherlandish Painting* (1953).[7] Panofsky characterizes van Eyck's art in a general way along the following lines:

1. The paintings by Jan van Eyck resemble and function as precious objects, like mounted jewels.
2. The paintings are reconstructions, of some kind, of the first creation (God's creation of Nature). They realise a "second" creation, letting the viewer become a participant in this process of creation.

The Arnolfini Portrait by Jan van Eyck, 1434, panel, 84.5 × 62.4. National Gallery, London

In his discussion of the creation theme, Panofsky notes that van Eyck's painting skill either informs us of a whole not fully differentiated, or of details not fully unified (181). The represented world is shown simultaneously through a telescope and a microscope (182). Among the characteristics of van Eyck's paintings pointed out by Panofsky there are also faults or shortcomings; the paintings seem to significantly lack the merits of Italian and classic art: the "moving" bodies – the centres of action and the preconditions of "great" art since classical times[8] – can be rendered properly neither by the telescope of van Eyck, which reduces them, nor by his microscope, which turns them into uncontrollable and immense universes.[9]

When he initially gives some clues to his own experiences as a viewer (180), Panofsky anticipates the main themes which recur in his interpretive summaries. He mentions the strong impression of luminosity (corresponding to the jewel theme) and the impression of minuteness (corresponding to the creation theme).

In this connection he confesses that the paintings do not appear to him as paintings, but as "reality" (180). This statement serves to confirm the creation theme, emphatically, but it also serves to single out van Eyck's paintings from the corpus of Netherlandish painting of this period as a whole. Other paintings, aspiring to illusions of reality, now change into lifeless items. Van Eyck shows us something "real," whereas other painters merely make pictures.

Panofsky extends this account by introducing yet another simile: "From the sheer sensuous beauty of a genuine Jan van Eyck there emanates a strange fascination not unlike that which we experience when permitting ourselves to be hypnotized by precious stones or when looking into deep water" (180). This simile depicts for us the following situation: the person stands gazing at deep water; the surface is alluring, with the striking beauty of light effects, but it also awakens his interest in the unknown depths; beneath the surface the deep water seems immense and it hides in its darkness whatever we cannot see clearly.

The combination of depth, darkness, the sparkling of light and the hinted visibility makes the work of art into an instance of the "sublime," more or less in the way this concept was understood in the eighteenth century when it was introduced.[10] "Sublimity" belonged to an existential dimension (of death and extinction) more than to the realm of concepts such as "art," "beauty," and "form."

In the formal analyses of individual paintings, Panofsky moves to the realm of traditional "beauty," a domain of formal relations and "harmony." In the analysis of the *Van der Paele Madonna* he describes its "symmetric composition," he looks at the conic form and the compactness of the Madonna group, and he finds the figures "crystallized." He compares the composition with other paintings, to find patterns of evolution in the artist's production. All this is presupposed to be objective, on the level of a neutral "observation language" (in the sense of the empiricist and positivist tradition) – not contingent on the scholar's personal experiences, but still recording impressions empirically.

So the reader gets involved in two prestigious domains of art: the beautiful and the sublime. The reasoned or "objective" arguments concern the beautiful and the compositional. The personal and subjective is in Panofsky's case tied to the sublime; it is not dependent on "evidence" in the formal composition of the painting. The sublime tone of the initial passages suggests the promise of an existential experience and an extended vision through the further reading of the text.

The jewel theme and the creation theme, the more powerful interpretive conjectures, are contingent on the subjective approach and the deep-water simile. The contexts and the arguments for these all-embracing judgments are not really provided (Panofsky provides contexts only for the historical interpretation of the marriage transaction depicted in the *Arnolfini Portrait*). The relational pattern that he establishes to confirm that van Eyck's works function as jewels and as a second creation is never made explicit, but I take it to be as follows: the paintings are visible tokens or examples of how we (represented by Panofsky) react to visual stimuli and the way we expect a normal depiction to exclude a fusing of telescopic and microscopic vision (this is the reason for his idea of a "second reality"; it could not be "our" reality, since it is paradoxical, but it has to be a "reality" because it gives the impression of being "real" and not "painted").

The next case to be considered is Otto Pächt's *Van Eyck: Der Begründer der altniederländischen Malerei* (1989, a later edition of a 1972 publication; the 1972 text was a revision of lectures originally held in 1965/66). Pächt does not divide his commentary into one part that is more scientific (and formal) and another part that is more subjective, focused on his feelings and viewing experiences. To Pächt his own viewing is the basis for a scientific analysis. There is only one level of observation and reasoning and the statements are proved by way of the "obvious" characterizations of the figures and their body language. Pächt does not talk about his own impressions, since these impressions are taken to be objectified in the picture itself.

Pächt repeatedly attacks the tendency to look for "disguised symbolism" in the art of van Eyck and his contemporaries. This kind of interpretive strategy – identifying glass bowls and candles as Marian symbols, for instance – had become the hallmark of the Panofskyan school, although it was actually not the final goal of Panofsky's own research.[11]

To Pächt, van Eyck's accomplishment is not a pictorial theology, it is not the invention of oil painting, and it is not the use of perspective in any mathematical or systematic way. Instead, he wants to highlight van Eyck's art as the first mature expression of a new world view and a new outlook responding to the beauty of visible reality, a beauty conceived as independent of metaphysics and independent of all sorts of ideological fetters.[12]

This attitude, ascribed to van Eyck, is "passive," says Pächt (24 and passim). The kind of awareness it entails is a withdrawal from touching and grasping to the mere registration of an appearance: it is an "appeasement of all the motory energies in vision" (24).[13] Strangely enough, to Pächt both looking and depicting are motionless and passive, more states of mind than activity. (It seems to me that Pächt thinks of looking as "not-grasping," that is to say a former impulse to take possession is given up and replaced by a substitute, whereby the substitute is inflamed, as it were, with the intensity of the grasp it is substituted for, although it is also "appeased" and literally without motion. On the whole this has a psychoanalytical touch, but Pächt gives no further references for his ways of thinking.)

This is the fundamental attitude of Pächt's writing, and it imbues his accounts of specific paintings. One cannot say whether to him the paintings' appearances are the prerequisites for his thesis or the results of it, but the two aspects obviously sustain each other and he gives no further evidence in justification.

The *Arnolfini Portrait* appears to Pächt in the following way. The discussion of the painting comes in the context of "interiors," and he notices how van Eyck has advanced from the tradition of earlier generalized depictions of domestic settings, towards the private, individual, and particular (and hence towards the historical) in the room of the Arnolfinis.

He then goes on to describe the figures as, above all, without motion and without sound. He imagines how the models have taken their stands before the painter and that all their effort is going into keeping still in order to offer the artist his subject matter. The new and noteworthy aspect of the picture is that the models as human beings no longer depend on God or turn to God, but expose themselves and stand in relation only to the painter (106). Whatever gestures they perform are finally only the raw material for a painting.

Pächt then contrasts the bodily stance of the figures and the mood expressed by their faces. There is a "split" ("Spaltung"), says Pächt, between the artist's observation of the bodies and his attention to the mental state of the models: the figures are motionless because they are lost in their own inner mood.

How can Pächt be so sure about the "inner mood"? The mood has no name, he acknowledges, but it is nevertheless a modern psychological dimension. Judging from the figures' faces, what is there to say about their inner selves, their minds? Pächt draws attention to this problem of interpretation through his idea of the split, but he stops short of specifying the mentality of the Arnolfinis. The expressions on their faces betray nothing codified, according to Pächt. What he apostrophizes as the figures' lack of a culturally defined state of mind serves him then to postulate a "new" sense of an inner subjective dimension. Van Eyck is part of a great evolution, according to Pächt, but he is the first to articulate this modern, psychological dimension, and the *Arnolfini Portrait* is its first recorded instance. The art-historical narrative of the avant-garde is strong in Pächt's writing.

To sum up the way the *Arnolfini Portrait* performs for Pächt:

- The figures are motionless as a consequence of their being lost in a personal subjective mood.
- The figures are historically defined individuals, and their environment defines them as such.
- The figures' postures are only important as the artist's motif. They do nothing other than pose.
- The scene appears to be absolutely silent (this secondary impression is caused by the lack of motion and the impression that the figures are turned away from the busy world outside and absorbed in their mental state).

It seems reasonable to find two basic themes (maybe not easily compatible) in Pächt's account:

1. The depiction theme (the painting manifests painting – in Pächt's view, people stand still and show themselves and the painter records his "passive" vision), and

2. The inner-mood theme, according to which the function of the painting is to point to a new kind of subjectivity, to make us feel drawn to the vagueness yet pertinence of the faces.

Like Panofsky, in a way, Pächt projects depth behind a surface: the "inner mood" (rich, individual, subjective) behind the faces that might otherwise just appear empty or neutral. All this seems to mirror closely the scholar himself as he stands looking passively, recognizing the historicity and sunk into his own inner mood.

Pächt does not argue for his interpretation. More than in Panofsky's case, the analysis is delivered as a presentation. And, obviously, the dominating ideas cannot be detached from the viewing experience. The picture appears as a response to what the beholder wants to see there: novelty, subjectivity, "passive" vision, and independence from ideology (especially metaphysics).

The picture is considered both as an index of a (vaguely) historically defined mentality and as an example of the attitudes contained in this mentality. The reasoning seems to build on the "evident" and the "we," and the reader can only gaze at the set stage and listen to a message that is the only possible one on that stage.

In some more recent scholarly interpretations, the van Eyck paintings are profoundly fused into their historical milieu. They are not seen primarily as reflecting or telling, but as remnants, as parts of a series of actions they once belonged to. The role given them is then more metonymical than recording or even indexical. They do not reflect or convey ways of thinking or feeling, but they are small shreds, traces of their time and society – not necessarily expressing or formulating their causes, but just belonging to them.

In his book *Jan van Eyck: The Play of Realism* (1991), Craig Harbison establishes a chain reaching back to the fifteenth century: the interpretation must be a reconstruction of a former context, and this context contains the people themselves, their lives and their beliefs; the paintings do not express or depict or communicate in the first place, but are considered as items of change and negotiation. Where does this attitude place Harbison himself, as viewer and interpreter? Does he show himself and deal with his own impressions? The answer is that he does.

Harbison himself is, of course, responsible for the construct supposed to result in the reconstruction. So he starts by positing van Eyck in a historically defined perspective where questions of knowledge are paramount. Harbison contrasts a medieval belief in trusting the senses with the deductive rationalism of the seventeenth century, and he then locates van Eyck between the two. (Without any references whatsoever he states: "During the Middle Ages many people maintained that the appearance of things themselves was a key to understanding their inner truth and meaning.")[14]

Harbison announces a theme very similar to Panofsky's creation theme: van Eyck's paintings show us a second reality, a "hyperreality" which is, in Harbison's words, both perceptual and conceptual.

Harbison, again like Panofsky, also gives statements about his personal experiences, again with a simile drawn from nature: "Looking into van Eyck's world is somewhat akin to perpetually living through those crystal-clear days that follow a spell of rain or humidity." Then he labels van Eyck's work as "realism," a kind of realism that is "unnatural in its dazzling clarity and profusion" (17). The collision between words such as "realism" and "unnatural" occasions him to mark his own experiences as arbitrary in relation to the fifteenth century: what appears as "natural" can only depend on a "highly charged process."

All the same, he undertakes the venture of looking at the paintings with eyes borrowed from the fifteenth century. But, does he actually do so – or how can we tell if he does?

When he looks at the *Van der Paele Madonna* his eyes are supposed to act as Van der Paele's and those of the anonymous church visitor to St Donatian's, after the canon's death. There are three main themes in the way Harbison reports the painting's appearance, how it acts out to the mind of the viewer.

First, he understands the scene as a comic act. St George tips his helmet as an apology to the child Christ, for having upset him; St George also steps clumsily on the kneeling Van der Paele's dress; and St Donatian "stares somewhat grimly across" (48), as if he, severe and watching, were keeping an eye on the disorderly St George.

Second, the scholar also experiences the image as the canon's eternal presence in devotion and as his plea for justification. The institution of the lay canons was highly criticized, Harbison tells us; the precious objects depicted and the inscriptions of the frame (referring to Van der Paele, to van Eyck, to the saints, and to the Virgin Mary) all serve to confirm Van der Paele's contributions to the church in terms of wealth (to meet accusations about the canons' being rather the opposite, namely exploiters), to perpetuate his presence on the site, and to demonstrate the church's official reason for having lay canons: to guarantee the ongoing process of prayers – with the painting, this pious act continues to work beyond the earthly life of Van der Paele himself.

Third, Harbison argues for an analogy between picture-space and life-space. The scene of the painting is seen as a "compacted arrangement" (60). It is this compactness of the represented room that makes it comic, but (and this is much more important to Harbison) it also allows for strong analogies with the historical reality of the people involved: if the painted scene is narrow, it is so to let us know that Van der Paele's life was indeed a "narrowly bounded ecclesiastical one" (60).

Harbison's interpretation is highly contextualized, it brings historical knowledge into evidence (on biography, economy, the church's institutions, and so on), and he seems to want to look at the painting as at other things once belonging to Van der Paele. The "reconstruction" scheme then seems to function as a mapping of the situation in which this object was created and for what reasons. But, it can hardly be said to apply to the "eyes" he is looking with.

Among the three themes mentioned above, the second seems to apply to what we have been told about Van der Paele – but the other two, where the viewing experience is more obvious, apply to Harbison's own position. Furthermore, Harbison's initial remarks on the epistemological value of van Eyck's paintings do not seem to touch on Van der Paele's concerns, as far as we can tell; instead, they inform us about the situation of the interpreter asking himself: can I know through looking?

The main theme announced in the title of the book, the theme of "realism," seems to me to apply to the scholar's own outlook: his is an endeavour of knowledge such as he mentions that the paintings were involved in. In practice he establishes an analogy between what he is doing himself and what he ascribes to van Eyck, just as he looks for analogy between the painted room and the life of Van der Paele. The realism strategy of the painter works, according to the interpretation, as an ambition for substitution and presence (the canon is depicted as remaining present along with his gifts to the church), just as the reconstruction of the scholar is supposed to replace the old vanished meaning with the construct of the interpretation.

But, the picture shows itself to Harbison mainly as a comic act. How can we understand this in light of the epistemological assumptions announced by Harbison as being typical of van Eyck and in light of his own ambitions towards realism in the sense of substitution and reconstruction? There is, of course, no way of establishing this impression as an ingredient of the reconstruction. It is just a loose end in relation to his ideas about knowledge – van Eyck's and his own.

Linda Seidel has inserted her object of research into a large variety of contexts, in her book *Jan Van Eyck's Arnolfini Portrait: Stories of an Icon* (1993).[15] Her approach seems to make way for a plurality of appearances for the painting. It is "staged" as a marriage document, in the context of marriage ceremonies, marriage depictions or betrothal depictions, documentary narratives, and the practice of law; it is also "staged" as the result of the court painter's action in relation to his employer, the Duke, and to the models of the painting, Giovanni Arnolfini and Giovanna Cenami; it is, furthermore, seen in relation to its later whereabouts, its place in Spanish inventories and as the probable model for a later and much celebrated "paraphrase," the *Las Meninas* by Velazquez; finally it is seen in the light of eroticism and literary traditions on love and deceit (a "reading" going in a countercurrent to the documentary and "serious" tradition, established originally by Panofsky).

The painting adopts various meanings, as if working like a prism – and the reflections it makes are mainly caused by changes in the "categorization" of the picture. To emphasize this aspect in particular, Seidel starts her survey at the National Gallery in London, where the painting, an "icon" of art history discourse, is focused in its museum context, announcing van Eyck as one of the heroes of art history, in opposition to and yet in contact with the Italian Renaissance masters and the other masters of the Northern tradition, Dürer and Rembrandt.

Van Eyck himself, as an artist, is elevated and singled out by the "icon" in the museum context. The very same move also singles out the beholder. In the painting, as one of the main ingredients of its world, there is a mirror, where reflections of the couple (seen from the back) are matched with reflections of two other people (seen frontally as tiny figures). Seidel holds that position, as she watches. Through recognition of the two spectators in the image, she can be aware of the relativity of the position: it can be taken by anyone (just like the place shown as the place of the royal couple in *Las Meninas*) and it can be taken by more than one person at a time. The reflected beholders of the picture tend to locate the watching act in the past, as historically defined figures, and Seidel respects the "past looking"[16] of all the earlier contexts, but she is still heading the queue of spectators herself. As part of the motif of the picture she works rather freely with its fictions; one gets the impression that she is the director or the conductor as she moves the prism, with herself, invisible but represented, as the centre.

There are significant similarities between Seidel's approach and Harbison's. Both want to install the paintings as part of the actions and material goods of a fifteenth-century Flemish mercantile and courtly culture. In that sense both are striving for a reconstruction of lost meanings. Both regard van Eyck paintings as documents, as signed and sealed guarantees of value and of presence to be regained (and the guarantee of the value depends on the artist's skill). Seidel even inscribes the *Arnolfini Portrait* into a trade practice, as a pledge by which the man, Arnolfini, could later take possession of the real woman's body, the valuable reflection of which he already possessed in the painting. Both scholars stress themes of distrust, triviality, irony, and buying-and-selling attitudes – very much in contrast with the idealistic tendencies in Panofsky's formal aesthetics and Christianized symbolism as well as the speculations on the inner world of contemplation in Pächt's writing.

But Seidel advances much further than Harbison; she actually "becomes" van Eyck herself, and in this transformation she has a completely natural claim to whatever meaning he had in mind, once she has qualified as expert historian on the life at the court of Philip the Good of Burgundy. Here she needs the mastery of documents, just as Jan did in his communications with clients and patrons.

The scholar's approach entails both a claim to historical accuracy and a claim to subjective involvement of a beholder in her own "moment" in history. Seidel's identification with van Eyck is stated in expressions such as "he constructed his panel in such a way that the viewer assumes the position in which he once stood"; the viewers perceive "precisely as their now absent artist once did" (188). And even more strongly, in her initial statements: "The web that I weave functions, in a sense, as a complementary canvas" (13). This prestigious position is free for her, because it is presented as a position to take by the reflections of the onlookers in the painting itself (188).

The variety of contexts might have caused a similar variety of appearances. This is not really the case, however, although implicit changes of mood arise when a documentary reading is abandoned in favour of a reading based on narratives about the deceits of love. A light of irony and comedy (compare Harbison above) is cast on the solemn scene through these changes of the mood.

Accounts of the appearance of the depicted scenery and its figures are rather scarce in Seidel's book, in fact. And all the passages recording impressions of the viewing act seem to converge, in spite of the different settings, in the same basic pattern of roles, attitudes, and movements. Thus the scholar herself emerges as the unifier and the origin, letting her experience of the work sustain a whole range of secondary meanings.

At the start, Arnolfini addresses the scholar and arrests her attention. The stance of the couple in the painting is "confrontational" and their attire is "austere" (11). Seidel returns to the address gesture later and says that the artist has left traces of his efforts to get the greeting gesture right, in his heavy reworking of Arnolfini's raised hand and of his feet: Arnolfini greets the beholder and his partner with the same gesture (188).

Just as in Pächt's account, Seidel describes the couple as posing for the artist. But this is just one aspect for her (it is rather like a confirmation of her role as the stand-in for the artist himself): they invite her interpretation as they once invited the artist's presentation. She then elaborates the scene explicitly by evoking passing time and an implied sequence of events. She sets the figures in motion: the man has come from outside, from the street, he has taken off his outdoor shoes; the woman has moved from her *prie-dieu*, where she has left her slippers; she collects her garment, as if to follow him out of the room; he has taken her hand to lead her, not only to confirm his betrothal oath.

Just as in Harbison's account, a story is inscribed in the scene. Both scholars express in the description of the performance of the picture its continuation in the different actions implied by the contexts of the interpretation. This move makes it clear that the picture, as an object of interpretation, is not placed in a dualistic sign relation to its contexts (pointing, referring, symbolizing …), but is on the same level as its contexts; it is a part of the contexts. The interpretation and the performance are both levelled together. In a poststructuralist manner there is nothing to be matched, only chains of meaning, connected in specific situations of social relations. The only one "outside" is the scholar herself.

In the process of interpretation there are stories, narratives about the people connected with the painting, and there is the voice of the narrator, the scholar's voice. The increasing closeness between interpretation and narrative has given rise to a problem of distrust.

The theme of distrust in Seidel's book comes to the surface at the reader's own dealing with all the facets of the prism – all focused in the scene of the man greeting us and about to lead the woman. How are we to make head or tail of these probable disguises of deceit? Do we have to turn out the light of one of the readings or rather combine them? The message of the picture cannot be serious and deceitful at the same time.

In Panofsky's view, van Eyck used religious formulas to elevate and strengthen the scene of the union. In Seidel's "complementary canvas," the use of Christian imagery could very well be a way of levelling the religious content, as it appears as some kind of pretext, a cover-up or a disguise for erotic manipulations.

3. THE PERFORMATIVE ASPECT OF THE IMAGE

I have repeatedly talked about "performance," and "performing," in connection with the viewing of van Eyck's paintings, and the time has come to tackle this metaphor in earnest. The basis of the metaphor is the analogy, already hinted at, between the activities of a performing artist, for example a musician or an actor, and (some of) the activities of an art critic or scholar.

A piece of music may be played in countless different ways, all consistent with the written score. One may have different opinions about the legitimacy or value of these different ways of playing it, one might argue that some ways of playing are more "authentic" than others, and so on. But opinions and arguments about how a piece could or should be played are not the same thing as actually *playing* it that way.

I suggest that the attentive seeing of, for example, a painting may be likened to a *performance* of the work. The painting can be seen in countless different ways. One may have different opinions about the legitimacy or value of these different ways of seeing it, one might argue that some ways of seeing it are more "authentic" than others, and so on. But opinions and arguments about how a painting could or should be seen are not the same thing as actually *seeing* it that way. In the case of music the roles of the performer and of the critic are usually disjointed, but in relation to the visual image they are fused – the critic must rely on her or his own performance.

Now, the musical performance is, of course, determined by many factors besides the written score and the explicit opinions and intentions of the performer. The motor skills, the musical habits and background, the innate and acquired sensibilities of the performer all come into play and influence the final result. To know that a certain piece could be played a certain way, or even to think that it should be played that way, in no way guarantees the ability to actually play it that way, or even to play it at all.

My suggestion is that we should view the discursive interpretations of art critics and scholars as related to specific "performances" of the work, performances that bring many, largely unarticulated, perceptual, personal, and aesthetic skills into play. In our scholarly practice we may, of course, want to concentrate on those facets of our own performance that we think we can articulate and argue about, in a way that we hope will be accepted as valid by others. But the relation to a personal performance can never be completely erased.

This is the basic sense in which I want to use the word "performance" in the relation to the work of art – the spectator stages a performance of the work. But this way of speaking does not, I think, quite capture the phenomenology of the aesthetic experience. In a derived but important sense I want to speak about the image itself as "performing." On reflection, we think of the aesthetic experience as an active process, but from a phenomenological point of view it is more natural to take it as passive. When I stand in front of the painting I am "grasped" by it, it "takes on a life of its own" and it "leads me on." To be grasped and led in this way *is* my performance of the work, but I experience it rather as a performance *by* the work, as something that the work does to me.

The analogy between the experience of a painting and a performance of a musical work is, I think, illuminating, but there are important differences between the two cases, as well. The most important difference is that the musical performance, in turn, has to be completed by an act of perception – an act performed by the listener. And this act can itself be executed in different ways: it can be more or less attentive, informed, imaginative, and so on. One might think that this observation destroys the analogy – is it not more plausible to say that looking at a painting is like *listening* to the music, than to say that it is like *playing* the music? But the best way to spell out the relation between the two cases, I think, is to say that the act of looking at the painting is like a fusion of playing and hearing the music.

Perhaps I can make my point clearer by introducing yet another analogy: between *staging and seeing* a performance of a theatrical drama, on the one hand, and *reading* the play, on the other hand. The reader's task fuses interpretive work that, in the staged performance, is divided between the actors and the spectators. For the actor, the written text works much like the score for the musician – it sets limits to what he or she can do on the stage, but it radically underdetermines the actual performance. Myriads of decisions concerning emphasis, tone of voice, posture, accompanying gesture, and so on have to be taken by the actor (and the director) and then be implemented on the stage. What confronts the spectator is not just the written play, transformed into another medium, but a particularization of it, enriched and specified in countless ways. If you "merely" read the drama, instead of seeing it performed, you have to do that work of interpretation for yourself – fusing the roles of director, actor, and spectator.

To see a painting is, I contend, in some ways more like reading a musical score or the text of a drama than it is like hearing the music or watching the drama on the stage. To experience the painting, as it is meant to be experienced, is not only to be visually aware of what is before your eyes – a distribution of coloured patches on a plane surface – but to experience and to enter into the depicted world.

It is obvious from the examples analysed above that the interpreter is "present" in various ways in the expositions of meaning, and that the image is, to some extent, experienced as if "acting" its meaning to the beholder. There seem to be stages in the process of understanding a piece of visual art resembling performances, resulting from the viewer's imagination that he or she is "within" the scene of the work and confronting the universe of the image enlivened through meaning. These stages come at intervals, they are active in awakening a quest for meaning, in the early impressions; they do not, however, typically belong to an initial phase, but occur rather more towards the end of the process, when meaning is close at hand – as a result or effect of the identifications and contexts inherent in the web of the more conventionally based interpretation. The aesthetic meaning of the work appears directly in the "performative" phases of understanding.

The figures seem to have latent movements and moods, dominant patterns of "events" start to emerge, "temporal" side effects start making themselves felt. It is as if the picture could address the beholder in an almost personal way, as if there were a tone of voice and expressive gestures. The kind of effects I consider here as the "performative" aspects seem to originate rather in the treatment of the medium than in the themes; the way the elements and figures appear is conditioned by distinctions in the colours, lights, and material qualities of the substances.[17]

The situation when the viewer looks at the object and penetrates into its world can partly be described as the sequential movements of her or his gaze "touching" the different elements of the represented space. But such a description would probably not capture the interactive character of the "meeting," or the instantaneous, all-embracing feeling of looking at a whole scene while also "wandering" through it.

What is also very important in this phase is the way the beholder completes or extends the represented world, and this aspect cannot be identified with the path the gaze takes.

The subjective, the aesthetic, and the performative – these are the aspects that account for the intuitive, sensuous, and emotional contacts with artworks; and these kinds of reactions also encompass intellectual reflections, triggered, shaped, or coloured through emotions.

Why do we need the performative, once the conventional and contextual meanings are established? My answer to that question takes a stand in the account of my experience of looking at the van Eyck painting. The performative, entailing aesthetic dimensions, recaptures the wholeness of the represented universe. The conventional strands of meaning endow the image with its potential for "acting," but experiencing the "act" brings back the unified scenery again, where no part is really "silent" or insignificant.

One prerequisite of the image's power to perform is the interpretation. And yet, the interpretation is the process and the document that break the coherence of the image, its unified but unexplained status. On the first viewing – the performance that precedes the explicit interpretation – the image is full, unified, but to some extent "closed" or "dumb." Since it is never, however, seen without some kind of preliminary or intuitive interpretation, inherent in cultural habits and viewing skills, it is still to some extent accessible. But the work cannot perform fully without an interpretation. The second performance is the event when the representation is seen again, as a world, in an attempt to regain the wholeness and the all-pervasive character the work had when no specific meanings had structured its universe into one or several dominant patterns.

Let me revert again to the analogy with music. A skilled musician who encounters a piece of music for the first time can still play it through, *prima vista*. But that performance will presumably be very different from the mature version he or she presents to an audience after a phase of study, interpretation, and rehearsal. To be sure, there are differences between the two cases, as well. The interpreter, in the case of the visual art, cannot perform to an audience – the actual "performance" is a mental achievement – but only, so to speak, try to put her or his readers in a position to "perform" the work in a certain way themselves.

The performance of the visual artwork to some extent reaches backwards, recapturing a beginning, but it does so only through the elements of knowledge gained in the work of elucidation and explanation. The initial state is then far from being an ideal, a lost moment of intense and intuitive understanding. On the contrary, it is usually inspired by curiosity and some kind of fascination, but it is surely premature; it does not possess the fullness the viewing attains in the second or later state. The first state of looking at the image can contain elements of unrest, of an urge to continue the quest. The impressions given by the work stay in your mind. The state of involvement at the beginning has only potentially what it gains in actuality as the work becomes interpreted and then "revisited." On the other hand, the work will not in actuality fulfil its potential if the inquiry stops at some level of conventional, contextual, or intentional interpretation. In the performance new meanings emerge, visually and emotionally.

4. VALIDATION OF INTERPRETATIONS CONTAINING SUBJECTIVE ELEMENTS

In this final section of my essay I want to come back to the conflict that I started from – between the *rational*, the *discursive*, and the *valid*, as contrasted with the *subjective*, the *intuitive*, and the *aesthetic* – and approach the question about validation of interpretation in the case of the visual arts in the light of my examples and the above discussion of aesthetic "performance."

What is peculiar about interpretation where the object is a work of visual art? One important ingredient in looking at images is the phenomenological transparency of the sign; one becomes involved in the universe displayed. This is not equivalent to saying that the beholder typically is unaware of the difference between reality and representation. The imaginary presence of the beholder in the displayed scene is not confined to very detailed and perception-simulating pictures. In fact, a picture may consist of very little, just a few traces, and still provoke some kind of imaginary involvement.

On the other hand, the transparency of the image is contrasted to its opacity, its quality as a produced thing. The opaque status of an image does not exclude its being used for the effectuation of transparency. If you are not aware of the construction, you will not experience the magic, the allure of the fictional. A person engaged in an aesthetic contemplation is aware of the opacity of the sign and keeps both dimensions conscious at the same time. The performance, when the aesthetic meaning emerges, contains a synthesis of opacity and transparency. You become infused in the world on show, and yet you observe brushstrokes.

To discuss the role of the "subjective" in aesthetic interpretation, and its relation to validity and reason, I will have to distinguish some of the different notions of subjectivity that are at work here. I will indicate three such notions, and then go on to discuss their relation to each other, and to validity in interpretation.

First, we have the sense in which *every experience* is subjective – the contrast here is with what is "objective," again in a special sense, or "in-itself."

Second, we have the sense in which the subjective is taken as the *personal* or *idiosyncratic*. For example, ordinary visual perception is subjective in the first sense – it is a subjective experience – but there is nothing idiosyncratic about it.

Third, we have the sense where the subjective is roughly equal to the *intuitive*, in one of the senses of that difficult word – an opinion may be said to be subjective when it is not based on discursive argument, but only "felt" to be true. If it is, nevertheless, claimed to be intersubjectively valid, this claim is, one might say, based on a trust in one's own capacities as a "measuring instrument."

Now, how can these three notions of subjectivity be related in an account of aesthetic interpretation? It goes without saying that every interpretation of a visual work is based on a "subjective experience" in the first sense. What I have said about aesthetic "performance," above, is meant as a contribution to the description of that experience. Subjectivity in the second sense, as the idiosyncratic, is usually taken as something to avoid, in scholarly or critical interpretation – and I agree.

My main point is about the relation between subjectivity in the first and in the third sense. The perceptual encounter with the work will give rise to many thoughts and feelings in relation to it – and for many of these there will be a tendency to project them onto the object, as properties it is taken to possess. Some of these "properties" will be easy to articulate discursively, while for others this will be more difficult – some may even be impossible to "put into words." Some of these properties will be immediately obvious to any normal observer, or to most observers belonging to some "qualified" group, while some will only need to be pointed out to someone who has missed them to become obvious. For still other features it will be possible to give discursive arguments to persuade people that something they did not immediately "see" for themselves is, nevertheless, present in the work. A lot of the work of the critic and the scholar consists in the effort to discursively articulate and argue what are at first only given as intuitions, as subjective in the third sense. And, presumably, there will always be a residue of things that he or she will, more or less reluctantly, have to admit are not there at all, but "only" personal or idiosyncratic.

If my remarks about the place of the performative in aesthetic experience are on the right track, I think that there are some lessons to be drawn about how to evaluate interpretations of a work.

There may be many truths about a work of art that are, perhaps to varying degrees, *performance-independent*. Such truths do not have to be trivial or otherwise uninteresting, but they do not come to grips with the aesthetic meaning and value of the work. To my mind, it would be disastrous if we settled for a concept of validity in interpretation that limited, for epistemological reasons, the aspirations of scholars and critics to such aspects of the work, relegating everything else to realm of the "merely subjective."

Interpretations that engage the aesthetic dimensions of a work, the ways in which it was made to be used, are performance-dependent. As such they can be evaluated in a number of ways.

First, the underlying or induced performance can itself be evaluated. Such evaluation will partly be aesthetic, rather than cognitive in a narrow sense. Is the work, performed in this way, aesthetically satisfying or good? Is the performance reasonable as a performance of *this* work, or does it violate some conventional or contextual constraints that we want to uphold? Is it true to the original intentions of the artist – is it the sort of performance he or she wanted to induce?

Second, the articulation of the performance may be discussed, criticized, and improved upon. Is it clear from the description what the performance is like? Are the metaphors used to convey it apt or precise? Is it made clear that the work can really be performed this way – can we see the work "come to life" in the light of the indications given?

Perhaps few of these aspects will be susceptible to epistemic criteria of the simplest kinds, and one might view this as a danger that the critical practice may lose its relation to clarity, distinctions, and rules of good thinking. But musical or dramatic performances are not arbitrary or exempt from rational discussion, and we should not let the demands of epistemic purism stop us from trying to access the dimensions most essential to our subject matter.

To my mind there simply is no alternative. None of the four examples I have analysed of scholarly approaches to van Eyck's paintings is considered as particularly radical or out of the ordinary. They come with claims to scholarly objectivity as high as anyone's. And yet they all relate to subjective encounters with the work, to "performances" engaging the aesthetic skills and the very personalities of their originators.

NOTES

1 Robert Stecker, *Artworks: Definition, Meaning, Value* (University Park: Pennsylvania State University Press, 1997), takes an explicit interest in truth problems and truth conditions in his theory of interpretation. He favours critical monism – a potential joining of all true statements about the basic content of a work of art – but admits a variety of acceptable interpretations with other *aims* than looking for correctness (truth and truth conditions); as an *alternative* to "retrieval of historical meaning," intention of the author or the work's basic content, he talks of "appreciation" of the work (153). Pursuing enhanced "appreciation" is said to be "legitimate," and an interpretation with this aim is said to be "acceptable" if it does not build on false assumptions and if it is compatible with some facts of the

work – yet, an interpretation with this aesthetic aim is presented as opposed to finding correctness. Anders Pettersson (this volume, pp 53–4) applies the same sort of distinction: enjoyment, application, and subjective reading are opposed to scientific interpretation where truth *can* be stated in connection with intentions.

2 See for example a work to be considered later in this essay, Linda Seidel, *Jan van Eyck's Arnolfini Portrait: Stories of an Icon* (Cambridge: Cambridge University Press, 1993), 12–13; David Carrier, *Principles of Art History Writing* (University Park: Pennsylvania State University Press, 1991), 237–43); Jonathan Culler, "In Defence of Overinterpretation," in Umberto Eco et al., *Interpretation and Overinterpretation*, ed. Stefan Collini (Cambridge: Cambridge University Press, 1992); Michael Baxandall, *Patterns of Intention: On the Historical Explanation of Pictures* (London and New Haven: Yale University Press, 1985), 116–21 (interpretations have no truth claims, but remain proposals joined with ostensive arguments); Norman Bryson and Mieke Bal, "Semiotics and Art History," *Art Bulletin* 73, no. 2 (1990): 174–208, esp. 207.

3 Carrier, *Principles*, 199.

4 For example, in Erwin Panofsky's methodological scheme the structure is hierarchic: the pre-iconographic level and the iconographic precede the final stage, the iconological, and mistakes on earlier levels condition later results. See *Meaning in the Visual Art: Papers in and on Art History* (Garden City, NY: Doubleday, 1955), 26–54.

5 The obvious contribution of the description to the interpretation has led an experienced art historian, Michael Baxandall, to the opinion that "explanations" (his preferred word for interpretations) of visual art always relate to other texts (texts that deal with a picture in the way the interpreter and other scholars have thought about it) and not to the work of art itself (*Patterns*, 1–5).

6 Seidel, *Jan van Eyck's Arnolfini Portrait*, 10.

7 Erwin Panofsky, *Early Netherlandish Painting: Its Origins and Character* (Cambridge, Mass.: Harvard University Press, 1953). Further page references to this work are given in parentheses in the text. Panofsky is in many ways one of the "founding fathers" of art history. His first authoritative texts are from the 1920s and he was active for many decades (he died in 1968). His methodology, "iconology," has influenced art-historical writing profoundly, and his research style has in recent years evoked counter-currents as well as new applications and theoretical analysis. See for instance Michael Ann Holly, *Panofsky and the Foundations of Art History* (Ithaca: Cornell University Press, 1984).

8 Aristotle, *Poetics*, 1448a, ch. 2.1.

9 On the Italian prejudices of art history, see Svetlana Alpers, "Art History and Its Exclusions: The Example of Dutch Art," in Norma Broude and Mary Garrard, eds., *Feminism and Art History: Questioning the Litany* (New York: Harper and Row, 1982), 183–99.

10 Edmund Burke, *A Philosophical Enquiry into the Ideas of the Sublime and the Beautiful*, 1759 (first published 1757), 89–90. See also Immanuel Kant, *Kritik der Urteilskraft*, 1790, part 2, where the "sublime" is related to formlessness and the unbound.

11 The whole problem of disguised symbolism is discussed at length by David Carrier, in "Naturalism and Allegory in Flemish Painting," *Journal of Aesthetics and Art Criticism* 45 (1987): 237–49. There is no support in any fifteenth-century Netherlandish text for the symbolic readings, Carrier states, and yet they are abundant in scholarship. Carrier tends to look for reasons within the personal outlook of the scholars themselves, and he contrasts Panofsky's association with and commitment to the humanist tradition (turning him into a promotor of learned allegories) to Meyer Schapiro, who also played with the allegories and riddles, but looked at them as obstacle and anguish, as the constraints from the past (and consequently used psychoanalytics instead of iconography).

12 Otto Pächt, *Van Eyck: die Begründer der altniederländischen Malerei* (Munich: Prestel, 1989), 12. Further page references to this work are given in parentheses in the text.

13 "Der Rückzug des Auges vom Objekt der Wahrnehmung, die Stillegung aller motorischen Energien im Sehen."

14 Craig Harbison, *Jan Van Eyck: The Play of Realism* (London: Reaktion Books, 1991), 12. Further page references to this work are given in parentheses in the text.

15 Further page references to Seidel's work are given in parentheses in the text.

16 In this expression I quote Michael Ann Holly, *Past Looking: The Rhetoric of the Image and the Historical Imagination* (Ithaca: Cornell University Press, 1996).

17 Thomas Puttfarken, *Roger de Piles' Theory of Art* (New Haven and London: Yale University Press, 1985) pursues the distinctions between the conceptual in art and the treatment of the medium, as these aspects are presented and discussed in classicist academic art theory, and he labels the treatment of the medium "performance" (28–9). My own application of the term coincides to some extent with his, but I also consider the level of tentatively identified representational structures of a medium as "performing."

6

Some Metareflections

Staffan Carlshamre

The contributions to this volume spring from discussions among a larger group of people, united by an interest in art, in the interpretation of art, and in the relations between different types of interpretation. We came from different academic disciplines, but we also had diverging backgrounds in different philosophical traditions. Some of us had roots in analytical philosophy (again of different kinds), some in phenomenology and the sorts of hermeneutics associated with Heidegger and Gadamer, and some came from semiology. Others, again, were more eclectic. In view of the fact that we started from such different locations, and used such different means of transport, it was not to be expected that we should all end up in the same place – and we did not. What is more surprising is that, in a very real sense, it was group journey after all.

In this postscript I want to comment again on some of the issues we talked about, and place them in the context of a discussion I would like to carry on. I will start with some observations on what is involved in distinguishing types of interpretations, and in particular on how one might conceive the unity underlying the splitting into different kinds. There are several possibilities here, and it is obvious that we have not all started from the same one. I will go on to the question of how to evaluate a taxonomy: what are the "good-making characteristics" of a classificatory scheme?

These are questions internal to the project of distinguishing different types of interpretation, occupying the first section of these reflections. In my second section I want to come back to some questions external to that project, in particular to normative questions about why the project is worth pursuing at all. What sort of illumination or practical advantages may we expect from a heightened awareness of the diversity of interpretations? And are there no dangers involved? In our group there were always dissenting voices, raising doubts, most often from a hermeneutic perspective, about the analytical optimism underlying the basic project. I will try to articulate those doubts, as well as I can – ending on a question rather than an answer.

1. THE UNIFYING WHOLE?

A natural reaction when confronted with an array of suggested types of interpretation is to ask what they are all supposed to be types *of*. What is the unity underlying the multiplicity? There are at least three significantly different types of answer to that question, and I will say something about each of them.

1.1. The Word "Interpretation"

One possibility, of course, is that two phenomena may both be called "interpretation" and still have nothing interesting in common, beyond the label itself. They would be mere *homonyms*, in the Aristotelian sense. In such cases even to talk about "types of interpretation" would be slightly misleading – somewhat like referring to the brinks of rivers and to certain financial institutes as "two types of bank."

It might be said that sorting homonyms is not what typologies are for, and that distinguishing such "types" would just be a preliminary to the real work of demarcating kinds that are more intimately related. On the other hand, to start from anything but the actual use of the word "interpretation" would involve the risk of begging some of the very questions we want to discuss. To break the spell of the word was one of the goals of our joint project, and to do that, one has to start from what people actually call "interpretation."

In practice, of course, distinguishing homonymy from polysemy is not quite so simple. There are no clear-cut criteria for deciding whether different uses of the same word are merely homonymically related, or hang together in some more interesting way. An illuminating case, which surfaces in several of the contributions to this volume, is the relation between the *performance* of, for example, a play or a piece of music, produced by performing artists, and the *discursive interpretations* of artistic works, produced by critics and scholars. Are these "interpretations" in the same or in different senses of the word?

Intuitions seem to go different ways.[1] An informal survey indicates that the gut reaction among philosophers (or perhaps just among analytical philosophers) is to go for the homonymy standpoint – and who would be more expert at telling concepts apart than an analytical philosopher? Dictionaries, on the other hand, seem to favour the unified concept hypothesis. Webster, for example, gives this definition of "interpretation":

> the expression of a person's conception of a work of art, subject, etc. through acting, playing, writing, criticizing, etc.; as, the pianist's *interpretation* of the sonata.

In this volume several contributors make a point of the connection between discursive and performative interpretations. Apart from historical criteria, which tend to impress dictionary editors, there seems to be no simple way to decide whether there is one or many senses of the word "interpretation" involved here. And the lesson to be learnt is, presumably, that it doesn't much matter. If there is an illuminating analogy to be drawn between what the pianist and the critic does with a work of art, it is surely there whatever words we use – it is just a matter of convenience that the English language has paved the way for us in finding that similarity. And if the analogy, on the contrary, is misleading, it is just a piece of bad luck that the history of our language has made it more difficult than it need be to keep apart what should be distinguished. The real question is about the fruitfulness of the analogy itself, not about English usage. So, how fruitful is it?

At first glance there seems to be a deep split, of a categorial nature, between discursive and performative interpretations. A discursive interpretation is a *statement about* something; for example, about a novel or a painting. A performance, of a piece of music or a drama, is not a statement at all – it is more tempting to call it a *version of* the work, than a statement about it. And the disanalogy seems to be confirmed by the simple observation that there are not only musicians, actors, and directors but also scholars and critics of music and theatre. Surely, no one would confuse the functions of the performer on the stage and the critic in the audience – but would that not be precisely the confusion of performative with discursive interpretations?

But this disanalogy can be worked at, from both directions, and perhaps a deeper analogy will appear.

First, is there no analogue to the musician or the actor, in the case of the visual arts or in those forms of literature that are consumed (or consummated) by reading? Look at theatre. Plays are not only staged and viewed, they are also read directly, as literature. And the significant choices that would have been made by directors and actors still have to be made – but the reader must take the decisions for herself. Is this question ironic? Is this line spoken in anger or in jest? What does the speaker feel, and how does that show in his face or movements? Answering such questions herself, the reader, so to speak, becomes performer and spectator in one. And once this point is seen, it is natural to extend it to other forms of literature as well – reading is a form of performance.[2]

Second, the performance of a play or a piece of music can easily be incorporated in a statement about it. You need only append some explicit or implicit *claim* concerning the performance; for example, that this is how the author or composer intended it to be played, that this is how it would have been played in a certain epoch, that this is how the author or composer would have liked it to be played today, and so on. And depending on the type of claim, it can be confirmed or falsified, discussed, supported by reasons, undermined by counter-evidence, and so on.

If we put these observations together, what can we say about the literary critic? Like his counterpart the theatre critic he reacts not only to the work in the abstract but to a performance of it. But the performance is his own – to be a critic you have to be a reader. Unlike the theatre critic, however, the literary critic is alone at the performance and so cannot go directly to formulating or arguing claims about it. His first task is to indicate the nature of the performance to his audience, to get the nature of the reading across and put us in a position to repeat it. When that is accomplished he can go on to formulate and argue claims on behalf of the reading, discuss its relation to the work performed, its relation to other performances of it, to point out its value or interest in different dimensions, and so forth. And, just as many of the spectators in the theatre come to see the play, but care little for the critique, a literary critic may be valued for the performances he stages rather than for his claims or arguments.

1.2. The Concept of Interpretation

But let us put these worries to one side and assume that we have managed to sort mere homonyms into different piles, and then pick the pile we're interested in. The types of interpretation we want to consider, then, are supposed to fall under *a single concept* of interpretation. What then is the unity of a concept and how is that unity carved into types?

The classical way to understand this is through the Platonic-Aristotelian theory of definitions, as giving rise to a genus-species hierarchy. At the top there would be a generic concept of interpretation, and types would be distinguished by successively introducing specific differences. In this volume Göran Rossholm gives an almost paradigmatic example of this procedure. Just as Plato in the *Sophist* tries to capture the angler or the sophist by hunting them down the hanging branches of a definitional tree, Rossholm tries to capture the elusive notion of an "artwork interpretation" – and rests satisfied, at least for the moment, with "the observation that the typical artwork interpretation is afactual and that is has rivals."[3]

A pure Platonic structure of this kind is probably always artificial to some degree, the product of regimentation and stipulation. And Rossholm makes it no secret that his concepts of interpretation are as much made as found.

At least since Wittgenstein's *Philosophical Investigations,* philosophers are much less confident than they used to be that words correspond to essences – necessary and sufficient conditions – in this orderly fashion. And Wittgenstein's anti-essentialism is not just negative – he also gives hints of another way of understanding the unity of a concept, in terms of family resemblances. There are several ways of working out that idea; for example, in terms of cluster concepts or prototypes. We might see this kind of analysis as a sort of reversal of the Platonic procedure. Plato starts with the thinnest, most abstract notion he can find, making it successively richer in content, and narrower in its range of application, by adding more layers of meaning. The Wittgensteinian, in contrast, starts from a rich, paradigmatic use of the relevant word and derives other uses from it by deleting features from the paradigm. There need not be any sacrosanct core features that can never be deleted – otherwise this would only be a different route to the same Platonic structure. And there need not be only one paradigm, one central height in the conceptual field – other uses might become paradigmatic in turn, bringing features into the dynamic that they do not share with earlier paradigms.

For a purely descriptive analysis of a naturally grown concept, such as the concept of interpretation, this is probably the way to go – starting from some clear and typical application, proceeding to others by following natural chains of associations, and charting similarities and differences as one goes along.

1.3. *Parts and Wholes*

But there are still other possibilities concerning the unity that binds the multiplicity of types of interpretation together. They may, for example, be seen as, in various ways, interdependent *parts* of a *whole*, or as *means* to a common *end*. In the articles by Anders Pettersson and myself, for example, various sorts of dependencies between different types of interpretation are indicated. Certain more specifically aesthetic layers of the signification of a literary text, for example are not available until the text has been interpreted on various linguistic levels. And one might perhaps be inclined to point out some specific type of interpretation – Anders Pettersson's "interpretation of focal aspects," for example – as the ultimate goal of critical or scholarly analysis. In this way many of the things going by the name "interpretation," in aesthetic contexts, would be united as means to that end.

Sometimes one encounters an even more ambitious idea, namely, that the goal of critical practice is something one might call the *total* or *complete* interpretation. In this way, what we have thought of as *types* of interpretation would more properly be seen as *parts*, or *aspects*, or *moments* of that totality. When taken literally, this idea seems misguided in principle – why should one expect there to be such a thing as a total interpretation of anything? It seems about as plausible as the notion that there should be complete *knowledge* of anything – as if one could anticipate every question anyone will ever want to know the answer to.

The idea of a total interpretation stems, perhaps, from the classroom situation. When teaching literature or art one tends to start from the work – "We will speak today about *Prufrock*, or *Guernica*" – and try to elucidate it from various angles. And so one may, more or less subconsciously, find oneself thinking that only time and other accidental limitations stand in the way of a total elucidation, which would be the ultimate goal of critical practice.

Or perhaps there is another idea lurking in the background, the idea that the goal of a discursive interpretation is to *articulate* a non-discursive encounter with the work. And if that encounter is taken as something like a *total experience* of the work, in all its aesthetically relevant aspects, one may be led to the notion of a similarly total discursive interpretation that articulates that total experience, or some suitable idealization of it. This way of thinking is perhaps most natural in connection with music, where the act of listening seems to be a natural focus for every creative and critical process involved. And almost the same thing holds, perhaps, for the visual and plastic art, where sensuous involvement with the work plays a similar role. For literature it already seems more strained. Actually looking at printed pages may be a necessary part of reading a novel, for example, but it hardly plays the same role as that of listening to a piece of music. The point becomes even more striking if we consider reading a philosophical text – actually sitting with the text before one's eyes is obviously only a tiny part of reading a Platonic dialogue, the far greater part being taken up by intellectual, and for the most part clearly discursive, work upon questions raised by the text.

1.4. What Makes a Taxonomy Good?

Another question that confronts us when surveying a variety of different classificatory schemes is how to evaluate the schemes themselves. What makes a taxonomy good, reasonable, or fruitful? There seem to be two main possibilities:

(a) The explicitly formulated taxonomy corresponds to a pre-existing implicit classification. Its function is "just" to bring an existing typology to light. The taxonomy is valid if it succeeds in this, but no responsibility is assumed for whether the classification in itself is reasonable or fruitful.
(b) The taxonomy is expected to be reasonable, illuminating, or fruitful in relation to its object. What does that mean? Presumably that it can be used for making interesting descriptive or normative generalizations. Something interesting should "hang" on which class something belongs to.

The controversy over whether the feature of "novelty" belongs in the analysis of the concept of interpretation, or perhaps of qualified interpretation, can be taken as an illustration. Torsten Pettersson, writing mainly from the first point of view, thinks that it does – and his excuse would be that this is how the relevant community understands the word "interpretation." Göran Rossholm thinks that it does not, because he thinks that it would make the application of the concept of interpretation vary with regard to irrelevant and uninteresting factors, making it useless for formulating interesting generalities.[4]

For another example, look at *aesthetic* interpretations as a class. Is this a special *type* of intepretation? In some sense, of course it is. It may be provisionally defined in terms of its peculiar sort of object – works of art. But if it has no *other* peculiarities it is barely worthy of mention in the theory of interpretation. Is there anything very special about aesthetic interpretation? Much of the discussion in interpretation theory is certainly carried on as if the answer to that question would be no. Views about interpretation are imported to and exported from aesthetics seemingly without much thought being given to the possibility of essential differences. Several of the contributors to this volume (including Anders Pettersson, Margaretha Rossholm Lagerlöf and myself) regard this as a mistake. There really are important traits that set aesthetic interpretation apart from interpretation in non-aesthetic contexts. In Göran Rossholm's conceptual trees, on the other hand, the category of the aesthetic finds no prominent place, the essential differences being located on other levels.

2. *The Pale Cast of Thought?*

We have looked at interpretation from a typological perspective, considering which are the most important types of interpretation and what are their salient differences. But why is this worth doing? What insights have we gained?

We started from the observation that the theory of interpretation urgently needs an awareness of the diversity of types of interpretation. Without that, theoretical debate will always run the risk of getting bogged down in mere verbal quibbling, and good observations will be prone to dismissal by counter-examples, based on over-generalization. Interpretation theory needs, so to speak, to secure the *projectibility* (in Nelson Goodman's sense) of its predicates.

This need may, of course, be fulfilled in more humble ways than by developing a fully fledged typology of interpretations. It would, perhaps, be enough to be aware that there are different types of interpretation, and in each case to try and delineate the type one is interested in from other types with which it may easily be confused. Indeed, one of the lessons to be learned from more grandiose attempts at a global overview might be that *local* clarity, in the context of a concrete and particular problem, is all that can and should be expected. The question of types of interpretation would be a *memento*, an awareness of the whispered question "And how do you want this to be generalized?" – but not a theoretical problem in its own right.

If the issue of types of interpretation in the aesthetic disciplines is to be more than a cautionary note, it must be connected to other problems in aesthetics and the philosophy of criticism. What other problems? The discussions in our group, as well as in the more widely attended seminars that we arranged, have always, in the end, gravitated towards *normative* issues. What is *good* or *reasonable* critical and scholarly practice? What sorts of interpretation are worth taking seriously, and what kinds should one take up arms against?

2.1. Relativism

In his introduction to this volume, Anders Pettersson broaches the question of *relativism*. Is there something inherently relativistic in the awareness of multiplicity itself? In some ways perhaps there is. The typologist puts an end to conflict, or so it seems, not by taking sides and fighting an issue through, but by keeping the enemies apart. Instead of a conflict-ridden, but colourful and interesting, multi-ethnic community, we would have a number of cultural enclaves, kept apart by United Nations peace-keeping forces – to which Sweden would, as always, be happy to make a contribution.

In order to discuss these worries it is useful to note that the typological perspective separates questions about the validity or value of intepretations into two kinds, which I will call *internal* and *external* questions, respectively.[5] Internal questions are, of course, internal to a specific type of interpretation – what does it take to be an acceptable or good interpretation of this type? The external questions concern the value and acceptability of the type itself.

The worry about a sort of relativism being inherent in the multiplicity perspective might then be couched in the following terms. Once the internal questions are put where they belong – into the different normative frameworks, each associated with a specific type of interpretation – is there still room for a reasoned discussion of the frameworks themselves? Or are we left with a variety of what Jürgen Habermas has called "decisionism" – having to take decisions for which no rational grounds can be given? Are we left only with subjective preferences? Or should we content ourselves with describing current practice, substituting questions about what is *accepted* for questions about what is *acceptable*? The last option seems to be favoured, for example, by Richard Shusterman in *The Object of Literary Criticism* – once we have recognized the existence of different types of interpretation, with different "logics," there is nothing else to do but to await "the survival of the fittest."[6]

Fear of this nihilistic perspective is perhaps the main cause of the reluctance, which Anders Pettersson notices, to recognize fully the diversity of interpretive types. Interpretation is, as he says, a prestigious concept, which one would like to secure for oneself and deny one's opponents.

2.2. *The Independence of Metatheory*

Shusterman's nihilistic stance may perhaps be viewed as an expression of a deplorable *laissez-faire* attitude, but surely it has other, more commendable, sources as well. In particular, it can be taken to express a reluctance to intervene *as a philosopher* in the internal affairs of the aesthetic disciplines. Philosophers of science, nowadays, do not make it their business to lecture scientists about how to do their job. Why should the metatheory of the interpretive disciplines be different?

The same hesitation to take a normative stand, when it comes to the practice of interpretation, is evinced by Göran Hermerén, in his 1984 article "Interpretation: Types and Criteria."[7] Hermerén starts from the observation that there is an unnoticed multiplicity of interpretations, and goes on to distinguish a host of different types, in several different dimensions. Presumably, one important point of this whole enterprise would be that critical practice could benefit from heeding these distinctions, to avoid mixing arguments and observations that do not belong together. But when he gets to the end of his argument Hermerén seems to shirk this conclusion. Instead he offers us a model of current practice, a model where evidence relevant to different questions is assigned "weights" and combined into a unified result – supplying an "answer" that does not correspond to any independently graspable question at all.

What we have here is a particular instance of a general dilemma in the social sciences: that the result of a study of a social system gets "fed back" into the system itself, coming to compete with other sorts of self-understanding prevalent there, and ultimately reshaping its practices.[8] And perhaps Hermerén sees the dilemma more deeply than Shusterman. To "leave everything as it is," once you start to make distinctions, it is not enough to leave the choice open between the types you distinguish – you must also provide the option of muddling them again in all possible kinds of ways!

More seriously, the effort to provide clarity by way of type distinctions may not be as neutral or as uncontroversially beneficial as its champions take it to be. An alternative description of the practice, if it is accepted, is bound to alter the practice itself. And a natural question is, will it be for the better? One's answer to that question, of course, will largely depend on how one values current practice. I will try to describe a set of misgivings in relation to the project of keeping separate things separate, in this domain – a set of problems most clearly visible from a hermeneutical standpoint, in the "continental" sense.

The basis for these misgivings is the lurking suspicion that the hidden agenda for the analytical project is a scientification or perhaps a naturalization of the humanities, leading to a "disenchantment" of the text, or the work of art. Why would that be? Because one of the first ambitions of this kind of analytical project is habitually to try to separate questions of *value* from questions of *fact*. And, by a logic inherited from Hume, this will start us down a road that ends with a sort of "factorization" of interpretive questions into those concerned with knowledge and truth, on the one hand, and those concerned with subjective reactions and arational opinion, on the other. And the next move is so familiar as to seem almost inevitable: to usher the second kind of concern out of science and the academy, into the sphere of criticism and private taste.

At this point I want to sketch a contrast between a "hermeneutic" and what I will call an "objectifying" view of the aesthetic disciplines. According to the objectifying conception, the aesthetic disciplines aim to investigate an interesting part of reality, namely, certain sorts of meaningful and enjoyable objects, and how they are produced and consumed by human beings. Aesthetic objects are made by people (as individuals or in groups) and they are used by people – what the scholar studies is the interaction among people by means of such objects.

Within the hermeneutic tradition, the task of the humanities is seen in an entirely different way. The interpreter is not gathering knowledge *about* a process where meaning is made and used, a process external to the act of interpretation itself. Scholarly interpretation, like all interpretation, is *part* of the social and historical process where meaning is produced. The work is the contribution of the artist to that process, but its meaning can only be realized in an ongoing conversation. And that conversation – this is the central point – is not a "metadebate" *about* the work, it is a dialogue *with* the work about whatever it is that the work is about.

In this way, what the hermeneutic tradition sees as most characteristic and valuable in the humanities risks falling between the two stools seemingly offered by the analytical reconstruction of our interpretive practices. The objective stool, for facts, does not leave enough room for the conversation to continue, while the subjective stool, for values and reactions, does not offer any common object for reasoned debate.

2.3. *External Questions*

I touched above on the fear that tidy typologies might lead to relativism on the "external" level. To be sure, "internal" debates about validity and value may have much to gain from being disentangled from confusions with irrelevant issues. But what room is left for rational argument about external questions of value? The hermeneutic reaction sketched above may be seen as an answer to this concern – better to have a dirty dialogue than no dialogue at all!

But this is not the only possible answer. Would it not be better simply to bite the bullet? After all, the price for continuing the dirty fight is high – to fight normative issues under a descriptive cover, never quite coming to the heart of the matter, the points where one really disagrees. The correct use of the word "interpretation" should not be our heart's concern. Why should we pretend that it is, just to lay our hands on that prestigious concept?

So, what are normative questions about different ways of reading or interpreting really about? What are we relying on when we recommend certain types of interpretation and criticize or denounce interpretations of other types? To me, that question seems well worth thinking through, and one of the great advantages of the typological perspective is that it forces that reflection on us. I will end by hinting at some directions in which I think that reflection should go.

The first point I want to make is that external questions, in order to be discussed reasonably, must be placed in some normatively relevant context. In a sense, they must cease to be external. And ultimately, I think, that context must be ethical – questions about value, here as elsewhere, come down to questions about the good life and what we owe to each other.

Look, first, at the private individual relating to a work of art – a book, a painting, a piece of music. What would be our basis for telling her not to read in *that* way, but to do it *this* way instead? After all – she bought the book and can do what she wants with it! There seem to me to be only two possible ways to answer this. One is to appeal to her own best interest – her life will be better, richer, more worthwhile if she follows our advice. And the other is to appeal to her sense of responsibility to others – a work of art is not any old thing, one might argue, but somebody's serious work and utterance, something we should treat with proper respect, or else leave alone.

In the case of scholarly interpretation, we seem to have some more leverage, more context to appeal to. Everything that is "allowed" for the private reader may not be acceptable in a scholarly or scientific context. There seem to be very general norms about intersubjective criteria of right and wrong interpretation, which some would argue belong to this context as such. But the question immediately reappears, of course, on the next level. Why should we uphold and answer to such criteria? And ultimately we will have to open the question about what aesthetic teaching and research is for – what is good about it?

And this question brings us back to the sort of dispute that I alluded to above, between the hermeneutic and the scientific attitude towards the humanities. Is the overall goal of aesthetic scholarship to gather knowledge about certain interesting aspects of certain interesting phenomena (works of art) produced in certain human societies? Or is it to develop, teach, and transmit the ability to experience art and to benefit from the experience? Or should we expect the scholar to actually take part in the creation of meaning, making her own contribution to that ongoing conversation about the important things in life to which works of art themselves belong?

NOTES

1 Here are a couple of recent examples. Paul Thom, in *Making Sense: A Theory of Interpretation* (Lanham, Md.: Rowman and Littlefield, 2000), tries to give a unified picture of both performative and discursive interpretations, as

being species of a single genus. Jerrold Levinson, in a recent paper, "Two Notions of Interpretation," in Arto Haapala and Ossi Naukkarinen, eds., *Interpretation and Its Boundaries* (Helsinki: Helsinki University Press, 1999), wants to keep them apart as not being "literally the same activity" (3).

2 This is oversimplified, of course. There are many sorts of reading, and what I describe is a sort of idealization of one particularly important type, what could perhaps be called the canonical reading of a literary text.

3 I do not mean to imply, of course, that this is the only goal, or even the main goal, of his paper.

4 I think Torsten Pettersson's view of this particular matter is by far the more common in the literature. Levinson, for example, gives it as part of the "received wisdom" concerning what he calls semantic interpretation, that "[i]nterpretation standardly presupposes the non-obviousness of what is being interpreted." But you do not have to make non-obviousness or novelty part of the concept of interpretation, in order to account for this feature of how we use the word. To my mind it is more natural to see it as a reflection of a general pragmatic constraint – namely, that we usually neither ask for nor offer information that we have reason to think is already shared between all relevant parties – than as specifically part of the meaning of the word "interpretation." A classical reference for this sort of point is Paul Grice's discussion of some linguistically based objections to the causal theory of perception. Cf. Grice "The Causal Theory of Perception," reprinted in *Studies in the Way of Words* (Cambridge, Mass.: Harvard University Press, 1989).

5 Following a terminology that Rudolph Carnap used in similar circumstances, in "Empiricism, Semantics, and Ontology" from 1950, reprinted as supplement A to the second edition of *Meaning and Necessity* (Chicago: University of Chicago Press, 1956).

6 Richard Shusterman, *The Object of Literary Criticism* (Würzburg: Königshausen und Neumann, 1984). Paul Feyerabend used to argue a similar position on a larger scale. From a philosophical point of view there is nothing that privileges one way of doing science, or, indeed, of forming opinions generally, over any other. The only rule of abstract methodology is "Anything goes!" What is left is only to let the different approaches compete for followers, support, and resources in the open market of a liberal society.

7 Göran Hermerén, "Interpretation: Types and Criteria," in Joseph Margolis, ed., *The Worlds of Art and the World*, Grazer philosophische Studien 19 (Amsterdam: Rodopi, 1984).

8 Charles Taylor has emphasized this aspect of the social sciences in a series of papers, beginning with "Interpretation and the Sciences of Man," reprinted in *Human Agency and Language: Philosophical Papers I* (Cambridge: Cambridge University Press, 1985).

Index